The Autobiography of

RosaMae Woodward Sterling

I dedicate this book to the

memory of my saintly mother,

Anna E. Pittman Woodward,

1889-1919

Anna Pittman

ISBN No. 978-0-692-80316-5

Design by BookCreate
Seattle, Washington USA

Printed in USA

The author, RosaMae Woodward Sterling, was born November 20, 1910, and wrote this book during the 1990's and 2000's. It was first edited by her son, Ted Sterling Vasquez (d. September 2012.) It was then edited for print by her granddaughter, Lorna Holmes. At the time of this edition, September 2016, Mrs. Sterling is living in Poulsbo, Washington.

Prologue

Anna E. Pittman was working in the home of I.N. Clark when she met the Woodwards. The Clark home and farm joined the Woodward farm on the east. Malmsteen's farm joined them on the north, and Uncle Asa's farm on the south. Who was on the west at that time? I don't know. The Clark home was probably four or five miles from Latah. On what occasion did she meet the Woodward family? I don't know; but these neighbors were all friends. She mentions in her diary the tedious hand-work on her wedding dress. I wonder how long was their engagement.

Part One – Girlhood

(Pre 1910 – 1920's)

———◆◆◆———

One day in September of 1909, in Latah, Washington, Anna Elisabeth Pittman and Orace Clinton Woodward were married. Their first home was a rental in a duplex next door to her Uncle Frank and Aunt Rosa Pittman. The Pittmans lived in a large house with a surrounding porch and bordered on all sides by evergreen fir trees providing a windbreak and delicious shade in the hot summer months. There were eleven children in the Pittman family, but all of them were not still living with the family in the home place.

The front of the house faces west. There are two floors above grade and a basement or more properly a "cellar" where fruits and vegetables were stored for the winter. That is the way things were done in those days. Frank had a special place on the south side of the porch for drying things like prunes, etc. Self-sufficiency was the order of the day. The following year, on November 20, they welcomed a baby girl into their home. "Rosamay" was how my name was spelled originally. On one occasion when my mother went next door to visit, she lay Baby down on the settee. Uncle Frank came into the room pretending he was about to sit down there. Mother's alarm was extreme and was often commented on. She loved me! She wrote in a small baby book my various accomplishments.

Probably the spring of 1911 or in the following year, my parents moved out of Latah, which is in southern Spokane County, to the Woodward farm across the Whitman county line near Fairbanks, Washington. Fairbanks in those days was a small village with a Post Office, a general store, a depot at the railroad station, a big warehouse, and a school. This was about six miles away from Latah, so visits were less frequent because travel was not an easy thing. It was quite a chore to harness our two white horses, Fanny and Shorty, and fasten them to the buggy to take us to Latah. It was not a surrey with fringe on top, or anywhere. A hack was like a pick-up truck and did not have a roof on it. It was totally exposed to the weather, but it had a place to carry goods. They usually took the buggy when the family went along. The hack was parked in the barn. I do not remember where the buggy was stored when not in use. I was a little girl.

The two Woodward brothers, Asa and Alba, came to the Washington Territory from Canada in the spring of 1889. They loaded all their household goods and animals on the train, family and all. They acquired a considerable amount of land due to the Homestead Act, which encouraged agricultural development. Asa and Miriam Woodward started a dairy in Fairbanks.

They had children: Harriet, and another daughter who married a Chase. I do not remember any other children. His land adjoined the land of Alba, (A.F.) Woodward, my grandfather. Alba and his wife had four boys: Milton, Willard, Orace, and Norval; and two girls, Elishaba and Ida. Washington became a State in the fall of the same year. Apparently the family added enough to the population to tip the scales into Statehood—at least that is the way they joked.

Elishaba was my father's oldest sister.   She had taken care of their mother in the years that the mother was ailing apparently with a slowly debilitating illness like tuberculosis. After the death of the mother, Elishaba married an itinerate preacher, who (scandalously) had been married before. His name was Isaac Paul. He spent much of his time in a rocking chair. Did he have health problems? I don't know why he sat around so much; but Auntie did all the work. Susan was the Paul's oldest child, then Alba, Willie, Ida, Violet, John, and Joe-the-baby.

Perhaps too soon after the death of this first wife, Grandpa Woodward married again. This lady was the "Grandma" that I remember. I think that she was a schoolteacher, and she encouraged the younger children (Norville and Ida) to finish high school and actually go to college—which they did. As college graduates, their education gave them a wonderful advantage in life, as Ida lost her husband and had to support three children herself; and Norville became a County Agent. The older children of my father's family, Milton, Elishaba, Willard, and Orace did not pursue higher education.

(Before Tommy Snyder, son of Ida Woodward Snyder, died, he discussed how angry the family was with the Grandfather because while the grandmother was dying, he started courting another woman-somewhat higher in class–that he later married. The family did not forgive Grandfather. He spent his final years in Vancouver, Washington, and died in 2005–but I am getting ahead of myself.)

By now my father was grown up and ready to do the farming on his inherited 80 acres, plus another adjoining 80-acre tract for his sister, Ida, and one for his brother Milton, who was in Idaho. In those days, when the farming was done with horses, that was a lot of land.

His youngest sister, my aunt Ida, was in college. The oldest sister, Elishaba, lived on the farm with us. She did not have any land there like the rest of the family. She did not inherit any of the homesteads, but Grandpa always kind of took care of her. Although her name was Elishaba, my father pronounced her name "Lashabee." This seems to be an English trait in family pronunciation. Other words that caught my ear were: Ideeho (Idaho), Albee (Alba), Idee, (Ida), sodee-pop (soda-pop), Sylvee (Sylvia), etc. To me she was just "Auntie." I loved her, and all her (Paul) family were like brothers and sisters to me. We lived very close to each other.

In front of our house and yard was a big gate to the barnyard. Beyond the barnyard was another gate to the road to take to Auntie's–just a little farther. Between our two houses, south of the barnyard, was a large garden spot; half for the Pauls, half for the rest for us. Between was a row of fruit trees-peaches and plums. Papa had a row of blackberry bushes on our side of the fruit trees.

It seemed to me that Auntie did all the work, planting and hoeing their garden. She was always on hand at milking time to help and to take care of their Jersey cow, Daisy, who lived with our cows. This was in addition to taking care of a large family.

On hot summer days the two older boys liked to play in the watering trough, much to my father's distress. They would come in from working in the fields with the horses and the water would be too dirty for the horses to drink. So he would have to clean out the watering trough and start the pump and would take a while before those tired and thirsty horses could have a drink. One day Papa came home early in the afternoon and found those boys in the watering trough again. He sneaked up, grabbed Willie, and thoroughly dunked him under the water head first. When he could get his breath again, he went home crying. His mother asked, "What's the matter, Willie?" "Uncle Orace made me swaller my gum!" I've heard my father tell this story and laugh about it so many times. I was too young to remember it.

Violet was a bit older than I; Johnny a bit younger. We played together in the sand box under the cherry tree in our yard, or on hot days there were the tall swings under a double row of fir trees south of the house, which were planted there for a windbreak.

Susan, the oldest, must have been the baby sitter, and told me the story of Epamonotus over and over. Once she found me happily ripping out my mother's crocheting, saying "O'May crochet!" I wonder what my mother said. It was the popular thing those days for ladies to crochet these elaborate works of art to put on their under-garments. Their blouses were made of sheer material, so these works of art were visible and their beauty was not wasted. My mother did embroidering, too. As soon as I was old enough to hold a crochet hook, she taught me how. It must have taken a lot of time and practice, but I made a very simple yoke to put on a night-gown.

My grandpa and grandma Woodward were living on a small farm in Kennewick at this time. I was very small when we went there for a visit. How did we get there? By train? I don't know. All I remember is that my grandma gave me my first taste of a banana. I thought it was sooooo good, I cried for more; then later threw up all over my nice clean bed–much to my mother's embarrassment. I have never cared much for bananas since.

Another incident impressed me greatly, so much that I never forgot it. A warm sunny day in June, probably a Sunday afternoon when my father was not working in the fields, we three, Papa, Mama, and I went for a "family walk" to our garden below the barnyard. I don't know what their conversation was about except to admire the neat rows of vegetables soon to be ready for use. Papa found a plump, white turnip in a row of luxurious growth that he peeled and shared with us. I knew by the way my parents talked, laughed, and looked at each other, that they were very much in love and happy. Somehow this warm harmoniousness gave me a great sense of security–to share this wonderful place, and the turnip which they had created by their joint effort.

It may have been the following winter in February when I had to share my mother with a baby sister named Beatrice Lavette Woodward. I'm sure she still took time to rock and sing to me. The Pittmans were all singers. The rhythm of this song *"He's the Lily of the Valley, the Bright and Morning Star, He's the fairest of ten-thousand to my soul,"* just fit the motion of the rocking chair with us in it. Another one I liked, *"There were Ninety and nine that safely lay in the shelter of the fold. . ."* which is another story with a happy ending. Other songs were:

Oh Where, Oh Where is My Kitty?

Oh where, oh where is my little grey kitty?
I've hunted the house all around.
I've looked in the cradle
and under the table
but nowhere could kitty be found.

I saw a boy trundle
away a small bundle
and carry it down to the brook.
Perhaps it was kitty,
so cunning and pretty,
I think I'll go down there and look.

I'll take my hook
and go down to the brook
To see if my kitty is there,
And if I find that my kitty's been drowned,
Oh, then I'll give up in despair.

Your kitty's not drowned,
she's back safe and sound.
I've found her all lost on the shore.
So take her and kiss her,
but promise me, sister,
You'll not blame us boys anymore.

Another:

Last night when I was snug in bed, What fun it was for me!
I dreamed that I was Grandpapa, And Grandpapa was me.
And Grandpapa was me, And Grandpapa was me.
I dreamed that I was Grandpapa, And Grandpapa was me.

I dreamed I wore a powdered wig, Drab pants, and gaiters buff,
And took without a single sneeze A double-pinch of snuff.
A double-pinch of snuff, A double-pinch of snuff.
And took without a single sneeze A double-pinch of snuff.

As I went walking down the street, And he ran by my side.
Because I walked too fast for him, The little fellow cried.
The little fellow cried, The little fellow cried.
Because I walked too fast for him, The little fellow cried.

And after tea I washed his face, And when his prayers were said,
I blew the candle out and left Poor Grandpapa in bed!
Poor Grandpapa in bed, Poor Grandpapa in bed!
I blew the candle out and left Poor Grandpapa in bed!

My mother taught me this prayer:

Thank you, God, for all thy care,
For things to eat, and things to wear,
For Papa, and Mama, good and kind
Help me to always mind
Like Jesus, in whose name I pray; Amen.

I do not remember my mother ever spanking anyone for anything. Uncle Bob Pittman said that she was a manipulator rather than a disciplinarian. She read to me a poem entitled *Which Loved Best?*

"I love you, Mother," said little Nell,
"I love you better than tongue can tell."
Then she teased and pouted half the day,
'Til her mother rejoiced when she went to play.

"I love you, Mother," said little Ann,
"Today I'll help you all I can.
How glad I am school doesn't keep!"
So she rocked the babe till it fell asleep.

Then, stepping softly, she fetched the broom,
And swept the floor and tidied the room.
Busy and happy all day was she,
Helpful and happy as child could be.

Of course I wanted to be like little Ann, who obviously loved her mother best. I probably wasn't very helpful. One chore she gave to me was that of using a goose wing like a broom to clean the stairs. The feather point would clean out the corners real good. There may have been other small chores too. I remember standing beside the kitchen table watching her roll out ginger cookies, waiting until I could have one with a glass of milk. I still use her recipe as they are the favorite cookie of my youngest son.

My mother's cousin, Lydia Pittman, a daughter of Frank and Rosa,

Anna Pittman as a girl with her aunt Theresa (Stanfer) Siebeke

Anna Pittman with fur stole

Woodward household (l-r) Guy Williams, Ralph Savitz, Florence Clark,
RosaMae, Anna, Orace, Beatrice

Three generations of Woodwards

*The Minnesota Pittmans: (back l-r) Tina, Henry, Mary, Anna, (front 1-r)
Helen, Emelie with little Robert, Loretta, Robert*

*Grandpa
Alba Woodward*

*Grandma (Smith)
Woodward,
Alba's second wife*

Orace and Anna Woodward wedding,
with Lydia Pittman Williams & Norval Woodward

Anna Woodward and baby RosaMae

Grandma and RosaMae

Anna and RosaMae

married Ad (Addison) Williams probably the same year that my parents wed. They were especially close friends and visited each other often. Their daughter, Erma, who was a few months younger than I, seemed like a sister. We quarreled over toys–especially the privilege of blowing out the match when my grandpa Pittman lit his corn-cob pipe. We had to take turns. From Minnesota, my grandpa was the only one who smoked. Since he was a farmer and bee-keeper there in Kilkenny, Minnesota at the time, it must have been late fall or winter when he came to spend a few weeks with us, and his brother, Frank, in Latah. By late fall or winter the harvest is over and it is too early for spring work. Winter was for maintenance.

There must have been some of these visitors with us for the very best Christmas I ever had. Papa made a Christmas tree out of limbs cut from the fir trees by our yard, and set it up in the parlor. The parlor was not heated every day. It was behind a closed door from our main living and dining room. On the day before Christmas, the grown-ups would mysteriously go in and out of the parlor, always keeping the door closed behind them. After Papa had the chores done that evening, he built a fire in the parlor stove so it would get warm while we ate supper and washed the dishes. At last Mama went through that door alone once more, and when she opened the door for us it was like raising the curtain on a great stage production. Behold! Our Christmas tree was alit with real candles– much more effective and beautiful than electric lights. Underneath the tree was a doll-buggy with a doll, a little red table and two chairs so that my younger sister, Beatrice, and I could have tea parties, or sit and color. There must have been other things for other people, but I don't remember because my eyes were on these particular gifts. Of course there was no such thing as a coloring book. We colored catalogues and other publications.

Farming must have been a prospering occupation during World War I. Papa bought a model-T Ford, the latest mode of transportation technology, and retired the horses, Fanny and Shorty, as well as the buggy. He added a shop and a garage onto the pump-house. That may have been the time he put in the cistern up on the hill so that we could have running water in the house.

Grandpa and Grandma Woodward had sold their place in Kennewick and were living in Walla Walla. This must have been the cause of Auntie and all the Paul family moving away from our farm. I missed them so much and was so sorry to see them go. Looking back on it, I see it is possible that Grandpa bought a small farm for them on the outskirts of Walla Walla about the same time he moved there. They might have been adjoining properties.

We made a trip there to see them all. What a tiresome trip!–chugging along about twenty-five or thirty miles per hour on steep roads that were not only unpaved, they did not have much in the way of gravel or shade; only dust, and more dust. Ladies wore dusters in those days for a reason. We wandered south through the Palouse hills to Colfax, then on through the town of Dusty, and crossed the Snake River at Central Ferry at the Garfield County line, then continued southwest, to Pomeroy, through Columbia County with Dayton, into Walla Walla County with Waitsburg, along the Touchet River here and there through Dixie where we turned west, and then, finally, finally Walla Walla.

What a joy to spend some time with the Paul kids again, and see my dear Auntie. There was always some interesting project going on at their place. Once they had a little donkey that all the kids in the neighborhood rode. Another day they decided to teach me how to ride their bicycle. That was impossible. I never did learn to ride a bicycle. We stayed with Grandpa and Grandma most of the time while we were there. They lived on the other side of the city.

Winter was the quieter time on the farm. We didn't go to the barn every evening at milking time like we did in the summer. Occasionally we would put on warm clothes and go to see a new baby calf and pet the kittens. There were more animals in the barn then. We were not allowed to run around and disturb them–especially the horses. It was a huge barn with a silo in one corner nearest the cows. Hay was stored on the second floor with room enough to drive a team of horses and a wagon with a load of hay to be unloaded on either side. There was some machinery for cleaning seed wheat, our cider-press, and a "hack."

Not far north beyond our new garage was the root-house, where we stored our winter supply of vegetables and apples underground. The roof had a mound of dirt over the top of it. There was a door which, when opened, revealed a set of steps going down, which took you to another door into the insulated storage area. My father organized everything in it. In the spring, usually in June, he would have to clean it out, so that it would be ready for another harvest season. He would haul out rotten apples and old cabbage.

A little farther and across the wagon road was the chicken-house. Beyond that was a building we called the granary.   I never knew a time when grain was actually stored there, but there was that marvelous incubator. How could a coal-oil lamp be adjusted to produce an exact amount of heat for twenty-one days to hatch chicken eggs? I went out there with my Mama one spring day, and lo and behold, there were baby chickens in that incubator. She gathered them in her apron, threw out the shells, and left the rest of the partly-hatched eggs for another day. We took the babies to the house and put them in a box by the stove to keep them warm–just like Aunt Em in *The Wizard of Oz*.

Behind the granary was the beginning of our big orchard. There were lots of fruit trees–several rows of cherries: Bing, Black Republican, Royal Anne, and pie-cherries; and a couple of apricots. Beside the row of cherry trees, began the apple orchard. The apples were of early, mid-season, and late varieties. There were also a few pear trees. The apple cider we made from a particular row of twelve Shiwash Beauty trees was un-surpassed. I never had enough. My mother would only let me have soooo much, because she was afraid that I would get the "back door trots." A barrel of that cider was stored under all the hay to eventually become vinegar. Once, when my father went to check on the cider to see if it had become vinegar yet, he found the barrel empty. The hired men, who often slept in the haymow during harvest, had been sipping cider through a straw, and drained the barrel.

Just south of our yard, beside the fir trees, was another large building, the machine shed. It was nearly empty during summer when the machinery was out in the fields. Down the hill from there and out of sight, were the pig pens. Every day papa would carry two large pails of surplus skimmed milk and kitchen scraps down there to the pigs. He took the cans of cream down to Fairbanks, where it was shipped to a creamery in Spokane.

When the Paul kids were gone, Beatrice and I had some other playmates, Jack and Glen McCabe. They lived across the County road from our property. Those boys had a whole box full of such interesting toys: wind-up gadgets, and gizmos to buzz across the floor, and building toys of all kinds. I decided that they must be rich to have so much stuff. What did we do when they came to my house? I only remember one time, when Jack and I climbed the crab-apple tree when the fruit was ripe. We sat up there and ate apples, and threw the little cores down on Beatrice and Glen, who were too small to climb the tree.

All of our neighbors seemed to be special friends of my father. When these folks moved away to Thornton (Washington), we would make a trip there every year to see them until they moved from there to Portland, Oregon, where they still kept in touch a couple hundred miles away. Maybe that was when Mr. McCabe died.

I visited the Fairbanks School for a while in May when I was six years old so that I would be better prepared to attend regularly in the fall. The Fairbanks community was proud of its new school. It began with two high-school grades. Half of the basement was used for the girls' domestic science class which made lunch for all of the school. The boys used the other half of the basement for a wood shop.

Maybe the plumbing worked. When I went to school, it didn't; and we used outdoor toilets. The two teachers must have boarded out in homes, because there were no living quarters for them. Is that how I happened to know Mr. Hycus? He was a rather unforgettable man, who played the banjo, and did not have ANY fingernails.

Papa was the clerk of School District #77. He was very aware of the changes that had occurred in education since he was a boy and had studied under Miss Gormley. When I started school, Mr. Hycus was gone, and there was no more High School, no hot lunches, the plumbing did not work, and the two ladies who were our teachers had a small house nearby to live in. There was a horse barn for the children who lived several miles away and rode horses to school. One girl had a Shetland pony. I tried riding it, and bounced right off. The family that moved into the McCabe place had two boys who often rode horses. Their younger sisters, Hazel and Audrey, walked with me. Walking that mile in the spring was pleasant, looking at wild flowers on the way. In winter, it was not so good. If it was really very bad weather, papa would take me. That didn't happen often. When school was out that first year and summer came, the twins, Fay and Fern, were born into the family. Later their names were changed to Lillian and Lucille. I do not know why.

We must have had a hired girl all the time from then on. There were so many little ones to care for, and often hired men to cook for. Florence Clark was our girl. The I.N. Clarks, her parents, were more special friends of the Woodwards, and Mama worked in their home before she was married. I wonder if that was when she became acquainted with the Woodwards? Florence was now a part of our family to help Mama with everything. Sometimes she would comb and braid my hair. It just didn't feel as good as when Mama did it. But Mama had two babies that needed her. Little Lillian had eczema all over her face and cried a lot and needed special care for a while.

They were both healthy babies when Mama's health began to fail. Emelia Pittman Senske, eldest girl of Frank and Rosa Pittman in Latah, was her cousin, and though married to August Senske, she never had any children. I think the twins were old enough to walk when they went to live with Emelia in Latah until Mama got better. She was to keep them and raise them as her own in the event that Mama did not get well. Beatrice and I stayed at the farm. What the arrangements were between them, I don't know; and I've often wondered. The doctor came frequently that summer.

I was now eight years old, to be nine in November. Mama did not get better. Finally the Doctor said that she had an inward goiter and it would be best to have it removed. It was September when they took her to the hospital in Spokane. The next time I saw my mother she was in a coffin in Frank and Rosa Pittman's parlor in Latah. My world crashed. Shattered, how could my life go on without Mama? They sang *"There's No Disappointment In Heaven"* and *"Safe in the Arms of Jesus."* It didn't help at all! I'm sure we went back to the farm after the funeral and her committal at the Latah Cemetery. There was always work, and school, and school and more work in our now-empty lives.

It must have been late October or November when Papa took

Beatrice and me to Minnesota to Mama's family. This was the home of my maternal grandfather, Robert Pittman, Sr., and grandmother, the sister of Rose Pittman in Latah. (We have two Pittman brothers who married two Stangler sisters, and both had families.) The children of my grandparents were: Mame, Henry, Mama (Anna), Tina, Loretta, Helen, and Robert. When Tina came for a visit at Latah, she converted from Roman Catholicism to Evangelical Protestant, like the Latah Pittmans, and my Mama. This was a direct effect of the Azusa Street movement in Southern California which spawned Aimee Semple, and so many Evangelical ideas.

I don't know who took care of our farm while we were gone. I got acquainted with my cousin, Ralph, who must have been about my age, the oldest son of my mother's sister, aunt Tina; and also my uncle, Robert, who was just months older than I was. Ralph went to the public school because he was now Protestant; Robert went to the Catholic School. Because we were living with Robert at Grandpa's, they sent me to the Catholic School with Robert. Their rituals and catechism were very strange to me. The priest came in every morning. We were supposed to stand up and say "Good morning, Father." That puzzled me. I protested. He's not MY father. There was the catechism as well. Why weren't we learning plain reading, writing, and 'rithmetic? After much crying and protesting they finally let me stay at home. We may have been there for Thanksgiving. I'm not sure. But we were there for Christmas. I got the nicest doll I ever had there, and their holiday food was wonderful!

Papa, Beatrice, and I must have gone back home to Washington again, soon after Christmas. Then I was back in school at Fairbanks where I passed into the next grade. I don't remember who our housekeeper was. One time there was such a poor housekeeper that Papa and Uncle Bob decided that no housekeeper at all was better than she was. They let her go and did the deed themselves for a while.

Eventually Papa took us to Walla Walla to live with the grandparents there. They had a lovely home–a big house with all the modern conveniences, surrounded by lovely tall trees to help keep it cool on hot summer days, which are plentiful there. In the back yard was a lath

Grandpa Alba Woodward and RosaMae at Kennewick Farm

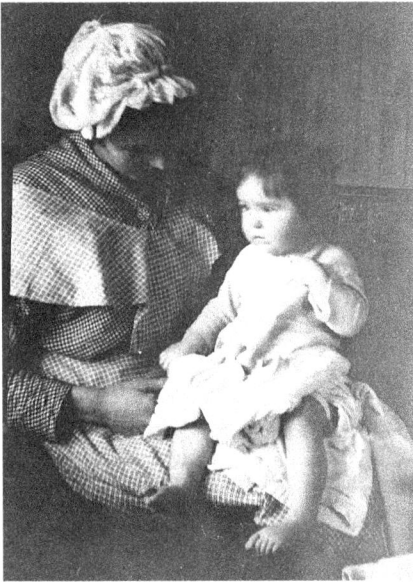

Anna & Beatrice 'I was just dress[ing] her one morning on this one'

Anna, RosaMae, and baby Beatrice

Woodward family portrait 1915

(l-r) Lucille & Lillian Woodward
(originally named Fern and Fay)

Beatrice and RosaMae
with book

RosaMae, Beatrice, Lillian(r) &
Lucille Woodward. On back ad-
dressed to 'Miss Mayme Pittman
1718 New York Ave Chehalis Wash
c/o J.Wasson'

School at Fairbanks; Orace Woodward kept the books

*Basement of Fairbanks School;
home ec class serving lunch*

*c 1913 'Mr. Hycus
the school teacher
boarded with us'*

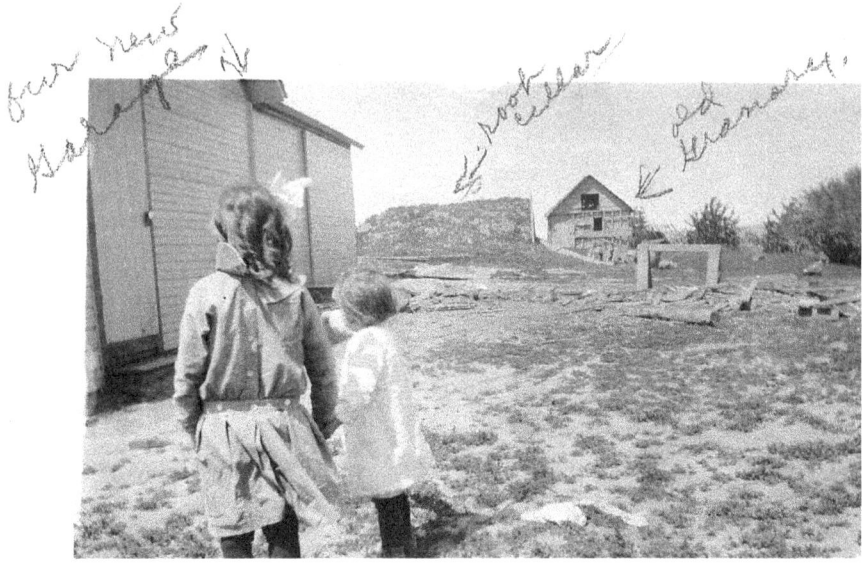

'Our new Garage, root cellar, old Granary;' RosaMae and Beatrice

Woodward girls, sandbox & swing

Orace Woodward with first car, Model T Ford

Harvest time, water wagon

Harvest time, men in the field

Store at Fairbanks with Orace in car

Inside the store at Fairbanks; it was also the post office

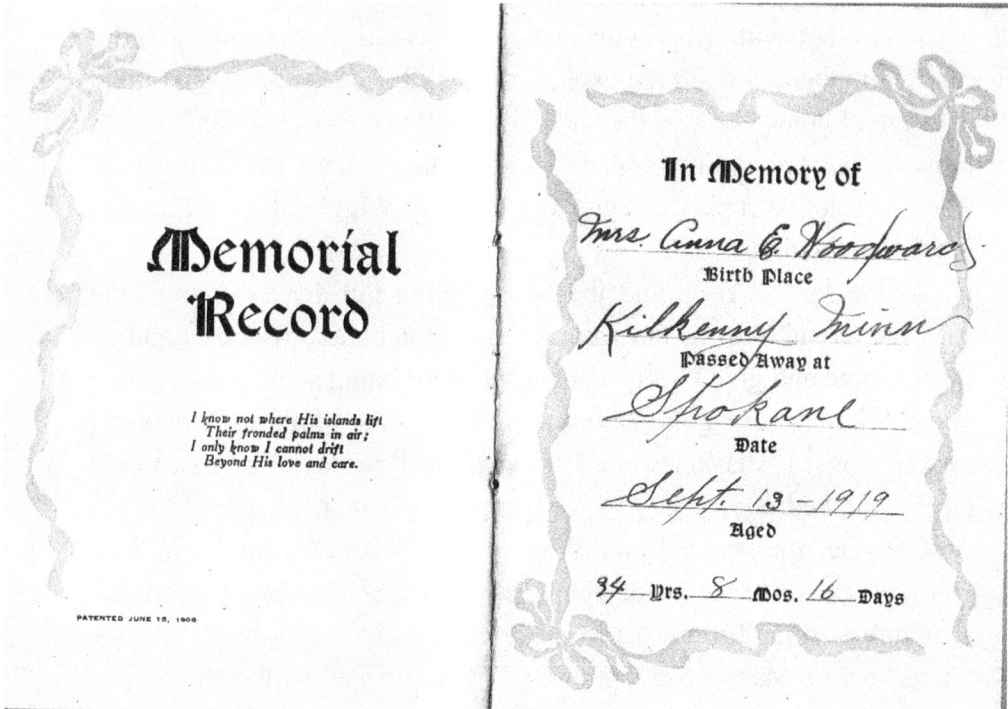

Memorial Record

I know not where His islands lift
Their fronded palms in air;
I only know I cannot drift
Beyond His love and care.

PATENTED JUNE 15, 1906

In Memory of

Mrs. Anna E. Woodward

Birth Place

Kilkenny Minn

Passed Away at

Spokane

Date

Sept. 13 - 1919

Aged

34 Yrs. 8 Mos. 16 Days

Memorial Record of Anna E. Pittman Woodward, d. Sept 13, 1919,
age 34 years, 8 months, 16 days

Winter in the Palouse

house covered with grape vines where we could play. Grandpa had a small farm there. We did not explore further. Beside the yard was a field of alfalfa. Maybe that was the hay that he fed to Crissy, his rather small, brown horse. I do not remember a cow, but he did have chickens. Every week he sold his supply of eggs to the Piggly Wiggly, the food market in town at the time.

As he drove Crissy and the buggy along the driveway from the barn, he would stop at the front door of our house, where Grandma would come and give Crissy a sugar lump for being such a nice, gentle horse. We may have gone with him once. In spite of all these pleasant surroundings, I was lonesome for the farm. One day Grandma found me in our bedroom crying. I was surprised when, instead of being sympathetic, she scolded me. "You've got to stop that or I won't let you have this nice room for your very own!" She got me busy doing something– some little dolls to make clothes for, or to the library for books to read. Many years later when I was plagued with depression, I remembered my grandma's wise council. "Don't sit and feel sorry for yourself; do something for someone."

Grandma was a school teacher and was always interested in encouraging students. She had an extra room where she sometimes kept a college student. Her brother, Leslie Smith, was head of some Agricultural Department at Washington State College, in Pullman, for many years. A building was named after him there. My husband, Theodore, and I went to see him once after he was retired and living in Portland, Oregon. Another Woodward was the head of the Music Department at Whitman College, in Walla Walla, for many years.

We did adjust to Grandma's life style which was different than our life on the farm. We each had cloth napkins, and napkin rings to identify the napkins, and we used them for several days. An Irish lady, Mrs. Carnehan, came every week to clean house and maybe to do the washing. I was old enough to help a little, like washing dishes or clearing the table, but I never did. I don't remember any neighborhood kids we played with, but I remember an unusual sight. It was a boy riding down the street in a small wagon which was pulled by a goat instead of a pony. It sounds like the last scene of *Porgy and Bess*, though neither musical nor dramatic. But it did serve to make the farewell scene using a goat-cart very believable.

When September came we started to school in the Washington School in Walla Walla. It was not too far for us to walk, but on stormy days we could ride in the streetcar from Artesia station which was a couple of blocks from the house. We never visited the Paul kids while we were living with Grandma and Grandpa. And they never visited Beatrice and me. They did live on the opposite side of town from where Grandpa was. If Papa came, he would take us over to visit them.

In October, Papa came and took us back to the farm and to school at Fairbanks again. Florence was not available to be our hired girl on the farm any more. She married our hired man, Ralph Savitz. Bob (Julius Robert) Pittman, another younger brother of Emelia and Lydia, was working on the farm with Papa; and he hired his younger sister, Lillian, to keep house. The school year must have passed uneventfully. When summer came, Papa gave me a job trapping squirrels. I was paid one penny each, and earned one dollar. You can do the math. Was I ever proud of that dollar! I should have had it framed.

Maybe that was the summer that I helped pick the cherry crop that was sold for two cents a pound. I was good at climbing trees, and that was fun. I fed and watered the chickens each day. The chickens were allowed to run free in the summertime, and often hid their nests. Their cackling would give a clue where the nest might be. On one occasion I was too late finding a nest, which was in a big roll of hog wire in the machine shed. That hen "cluck, cluck, clucked" and kept those eggs warm. I kept watching that nest because I knew those baby chicks would need help when they hatched, to get out of that roll of wire to go with their mother hen. Another time I found a nest in the dark corner of the hay-mow. One day when I went there to get the usual eggs, I found it occupied by a family of kittens.

We got along fine with Lillian Pittman. She was like a big sister to us. I must have learned to help some in the kitchen–set the table, wash, or wipe the dishes. After a hot day in the summer, when all the chores were done, we would sit out on the porch in the cool of the evening and sing–Lillian with the guitar, and I learned to chord on the ukulele. I sang soprano; she sang alto. I do not remember Beatrice singing, but I liked to sing. I learned new songs at school from *The Golden Book of Favorite Songs*, besides the many hymns at church. I often sang myself to sleep at night; but I kind of grew out of that. Beatrice and I shared a double bed. I could not stand to be touched accidentally by her, so a pole wrapped in a blanket was placed in the middle of the bed between us.

My family went to Oakesdale to a 'chataqua,' a traveling group of entertainers, where we heard a violinist play *Salute d'Amour* and other things. I was so impressed, I was sure I wanted to play violin. Grandpa Woodward gave me his violin at some time. Only once did he demonstrate his old-time fiddling for me. Many years later I gave up trying to learn to play violin beautifully, and passed his violin on to my cousin, Susan, who did play much better than I ever could.

Harvest time and summer were soon over and it was time to go back to school and once again start the usual autumn routine of storing apples and vegetables in the root-house for winter. The chicken-house had to be thoroughly cleaned, de-bugged, and the chickens rounded up, and shut in for winter. Sometimes they would roost in the trees. We could catch them at night and put them in the chicken-house. Because of these chores, I can imagine that it was late in the fall when Papa asked Beatrice and me how we would like to have Lillian as a permanent part of our family.

It sounded like a very good idea. In December we all went to Spokane, and they were married by the pastor that always came to Grandma Rose Pittman's every Sunday for church.　　Another winter at home on the farm where we spent long evenings playing games like dominos. We had a double-twelve set. We read stories. There were serial stories in magazines. One story in the old *Washington Farmer* magazine was "Ben Snipes: Cattle King of the Northwest." That was a true story. Our neighbor Clyde Waterman's mother met Ben Snipes. We had another book that was hilariously funny: *A Bad Boy's Diary*. There were others, too, of course. We used Aladdin lamps for light. They must have been a great improvement over candles. We once found candle-making forms in the cellar, along with the family cheese-making tools. Papa said that his family made extra cheeses–those big round cakes—for the neighbors.

Another spring and summer came. Bob Pittman was with us all the time–still farming with Papa. He was my dearest friend. I would rush to the door to greet him when he came in from work, then sit on his lap while he rested, rather than the lap of my father. (Would Beatrice go to Papa's lap? I don't remember.)

That summer we had another hired girl, Nora Michel. She was a great story-teller. She kept us entertained with long stories while we shelled peas for canning. That was such a tiresome job. After that, I began reading books for myself. Some were given to me as gifts: *Pollyanna, The Girl of the Limberlost*, and others. When I read *The Girl of the Limberlost*, I fantasized our expansive orchard as being like the forest that she described in her book. (The Palouse hills did not have any natural forests, so I had to imagine what a "forest" looked like.) We found out that Papa's cousin, Harriet, who lived at Fairbanks, had quite a library. She had lots of westerns, and we borrowed books from her. After harvest-time, Nora left us.

When winter came, we welcomed into our home a baby boy. Nurse Wilson came to spend a week with us and take care of the mother and baby as was the custom. Babies were born at home, not in the hospital. After having four girls, a boy was most welcome. He seemed perfect in every way, but after a few days he began to cry a lot. Nobody could find a reason why. As the days went by, it was frustrating to hear him having a problem, but not to know how to comfort him. After a couple of weeks he quit crying forever. Our dear baby, Orace, was dead. Modern medicine of today would probably have saved him. It was winter; the only flowers we could find for the little coffin were from someone's house plants. The twins never saw this brother at all, as they were still with Emelia and August in Latah.

Life on the farm continued with chores to do, and school every day. Months passed. It must have been about February, after her birthday, my sister, Beatrice caught a cold. She had to stay out of school several days. One day, about noon, the folks came to school and took me home to the farm. I wondered why. They decided that it was the appropriate thing to do, because my sister Beatrice was dead. I was told that she had bronchial pneumonia-croup. Another cousin, Annie (Pittman) said that she had polio. We never heard of such a thing as "polio" then. We all had to be out of the house for a day while it was fumigated. We lost several other children in the community that year. I do not know if there was a little epidemic and she was part of it, or whether she simply died of something else. I do not remember where we went to spend the day while the house was being fumigated. I do not remember a funeral for Beatrice, either.

When fall came I believe that I was in the eighth grade, my last year at Fairbanks School District, and home at the farm. Bob continued to help Papa with the farming. Life went on without Beatrice. I grew up enough for me to quit sitting on his lap, but he was still my best friend. I could tell him about my interest in the boy next door, Ross Harris was his name; and he told me about his latest girl-friend–a very attractive new-comer to Latah, Ruth Allen. He had other girl friends; I have pictures of him with them.

Having read about romances in many books by this time, real-life ones interested me, too. I heard about Bob's youngest sister, Adeline, going out with Irvin Savitz, brother of Ralph. That affair did not last long, as I never saw them together.

It may have been sometime this year that Emelia decided that the twins should live with their father and his new wife. When I come to this point of the story, I hesitate and wonder just what the agreement was with our Mother. We'll never know. Maybe she was tired of taking care of little ones. Were they there in time to start to school? Perhaps. I don't know. My sister, Lillian, remembers being back there on the farm the following January when another baby boy was born into our home. He, Clinton, did not live as long as little Orace. She went and told "Mom" (Lillian Pittman) that she was sorry.

Bob must have left us by this time, and he married Ruth, to have his own home and farm, the Nelson place–a farm that was about half-way between our farm and Latah. I will discuss the Nelsons later. Was this the year I finished the eighth grade? I am not sure. One Christmas I got a manicure set instead of a book; that certainly was a disappointment. I do not remember playing with the twins–or spending any time with them– even when we must have been living in the same place at the same time again at last. Things were happening in Latah that would further affect my life.

Ed Pittman was the second-oldest son of Frank and Rose; rather wiry and parted his hair a little off center in Edwardian fashion. He was another brother to Emelia, Lydia, Bob, and Lillian. (It was a big family and you are going to meet them all. They were divided into the "first family": Joe, Emelia, Ed, Lydia, Rose, Emil; and the "second family": Gustaff (Frank), Bob, Bill, Lillian, Adeline. There was a period of years between these families even though the parents were exactly the same.) Ed and his wife, Bertha, sometimes provided room and board for the local school teachers. This year they had a be-spectacled, young graduate of Washington State College in Pullman who came to teach at Latah High School. His name was Sherman R. Sterling.

Apparently Adeline, the baby of the Pittman family, had broken up with Irvin Savitz, so that both were back on the romance market again. I do not know how they ever got acquainted or any of the events of their courting ritual there, but Sherm and Adeline became a married couple. Since Fairbanks School only went to the eighth grade, my first year of high school I lived with them. They had two children by that time, Ross and Glenna, so they wanted some help with the extra washing and ironing. It may have been the second winter that I was with them that they had another boy they named Glen, who died of pneumonia.

My third year of high school, I spent with August and Emelia. Not as much to do there–just help with the house-cleaning; but she was a hard taskmaster, and difficult to please. She had every known convenience of the day–an electric range and refrigerator, indoor plumbing, a furnace in the basement instead of a heating stove in the living room. One day her husband, August, came home and dropped his felt hat on top of the refrigerator instead of the coat-rack nearby. "Oh! You mustn't do that! It might scratch the refrigerator." I think I remembered that because I thought it was so unreasonable.

It may have been that summer when I went home to the farm after school that I found things were different there. The garden was not being taken care of; it was full of weeds. I thought of Mama and the turnip. If she were here, it would not be like this. I weeded out a long row of beets while praying that God would weed out every undesirable thing in my life so that some day I could be with Him and my mother again–in Heaven.

My father must have been having financial difficulties that I was not aware of. Were the crops poor? He worked in the Warehouse at Fairbanks to earn extra money when he could. Mom (Lillian) would complain and criticize everything that he did. On one occasion he simply resigned and said, "Okay. You run things; I'm leaving." He walked out to the garage to the car. She and I were both crying. We ran to him and begged him not to go away, and he came back.

It may have been that summer that I spent the weeks of harvest-time in Latah with the Williams family. Erma, Sherman, and Lorraine are the children of Ad and Lydia (Pittman.) Lydia and her oldest daughter, Erma, were cooking for the harvest men in a cook-wagon out in the fields. I kept the house clean, the other children fed, and did their washing. Sherman and Lorraine were school-aged, well-behaved, and pleasant to be with.

Another summer I worked for Bob and Ruth Pittman. Their son,

Leighton, was a baby. Ruth was quite a contrast to the Pittman women. She was so sweet to me and taught me to make bread, and probably other things. Bob decided that he would make some cherry wine. He filled a big crock with sweet cherries and sugar; then set it aside to ferment. It did; but I don't think it ever turned into wine. What a mess!

When school started in the fall, I went to live with the oldest and largest Pittman brother, Joe, and his wife, Mary, in their home at Latah. They had three children of their own: Arnetta, the oldest, Carl, who was about my age, and Aura, a younger girl. Joe was physically a commanding presence–a big, strong man. He sang bass, parted his hair in the middle, and even looked like he belonged in a barbershop quartet. My father must have paid something for my room and board. I was not much help there. I remember one time Arnetta coming home from a trip to Spokane with a brand new piece of sheet music she bought, *Bye Bye, Blackbird*. Needless to say, eyebrows rose; but Arnetta did not care about local eyebrows then– and never did. I shared a room with Lucille Fetzner. She was a good friend whose parents lived in the Fairbanks area.

At school, Sherm Sterling had advanced to being the principal of Latah High School. He was my Physics teacher. I probably did about average in all of my classes. I probably could have done better if I had not been so involved with my social life–boys. The ones that I liked never were interested in me. I did not go to ball games or dances. Those things were considered "worldly" by the (Evangelical) Pittmans. I only went to church. So I walked to church with one special boy, Walter Krell, sat there with him, and then walked home again. Once was enough. Next was Leonard Clark. I do not remember where I met him. He was not related to the Clarks that we knew on the farm. We were together for several months. He brought me candy, just too much–a lovely valentine box.

That spring Carl Pittman persuaded his mother to let him use the car to take his girl-friend on a date. Leonard and I went along, too. When it was time to go home, we let off the girl at her place. I do not remember just who she was now. Then we dropped off Leonard at his place, and then we went on home alone. This happened several times. Carl and I found that we liked each other's company the best. Another time we left our dates at home and went to a movie together in Tekoa, a town just over the county line in Palouse County, further east than Fairbanks. What a sinful episode! That was the first movie I ever saw. It was a Nelson Eddy/ Jeanette McDonald musical.

Church was interesting, too. At that time (my last year in high school), William E. Booth-Clibborn was having special Evangelistic meetings in Spokane. He was a relative of the Booths or Clibborns who started the Salvation Army, and was a well-known evangelist at the time. The Booths and Clibborns put new lyrics to classy opera arias, and serious classical music, making hymns out of them–a step up from Wesley hymns. He played the violin beautifully! Someone from Latah would take a load of young folks from our church to attend. I went as often as I could. The music impressed me. Clibborn played the violin with most of the singing. I still have a song book that I bought from there with some of his compositions in it.

Another occasion I went to a "camp meeting" with Bob and Ruth. It was on the eastern outskirts of Portland, Oregon. This must have been before they had any children. There was a new and beautiful highway opened through the Columbia River Gorge. I remember going by Celilo Falls, where the Indians camped and fished. We stopped at the Vista House for the spectacular view of the Gorge. (Now only a part of that road remains.) We passed a Catholic Shrine (The Sanctuary of Our Sorrowful Mother) on our way west toward Portland to the campsite. It was near enough so that we could walk back several blocks and visit the Sanctuary. I don't know how long we were there. It was quite a trip.

A family from Spokane came to visit our church in Latah occasionally, and treated us with "special" music. The oldest child, a teenaged girl, played violin. The three boys played wind instruments. They played instrumental ensembles. Sometimes "Mom" and I would sing a duet. Erma would sing "*Whispering Hope*" with me.

Actually my interest in music started much earlier, when I slept with Beatrice, and continued through "Mom" and our singing together on the farm. She had taken voice lessons in Spokane from a student of Amelita Galli-Curci, the famous opera singer. We had such a good selection of phonograph records on the farm that I listened to. There were two that I especially remember and tried to imitate: *Un Bel Di* from *Madame*

Butterfly, and *The Wren*. Boy! I wish I could hear somebody do that one now. I have not heard it since Lily Pons recorded it in the late 1940's.

This is kind of a puzzle to me–it must have been one of these summers that I had a few piano lessons. We did not have a piano, only a "pump organ." I had lessons from Mrs. Helmer, but never had a piano to practice. I learned what the notes were to tune the violin to. I do not remember a piano in Latah with Sherm and Adeline. Joe and Ed Pittman both had pianos. Sherm and Adeline got a piano later. Adeline had a piano at Frank and Rose Pittman's house. (Bethel practiced on it when she was a girl.) Lydia had a mandolin, but I never knew anyone to play it. Frank must have played the violin. The Pittman family got together on Sunday afternoons to make music. There was a LOT of singers. Joe played harmonica. If you could not play something, you were expected to sing.

I graduated from Latah High School in the Class of 1929. It was not a big deal. There was no school for me that fall. Instead I went to work in Dr. Nelson's home in Tekoa. Bob Pittman was managing Dr. Nelson's farm at the time. Mrs. Nelson was recovering from an operation. I was supposed to do the "heavier" work, like washing, cooking, and cleaning. That was easy for me. Their two children were in college and sent their washing home. Marjorie was a senior, and John was a freshman; both were at Washington State College in Pullman. With only three adults in their beautiful, big, house, it was easy to keep clean. There wasn't much work to do. I had time to spare, and I asked Mrs. Nelson if she would mind if I took some piano lessons. YES. So I did; I took some lessons. I also learned to cook things that he liked. One day he did not feel very well and asked me to make some milk-toast. He had to tell me how to do that because I had never heard of it.

The big football game during Thanksgiving week between Washington State College and the University of Washington was the really big sporting event of the season. Mrs. Nelson and I went to Pullman and spent the week-end with Marjorie in her sorority house. That is as close as I ever came to attending college myself.

Sherm Sterling was not in Latah any more. He had moved to Coulee City, Washington, where he had another school, and they were living there. Adeline kept coaxing me to come and live with her there in Coulee City. She still had two children. Finally, in December, I quit my job, recommended my friend Lucille Fetzner for my replacement, and went to Coulee City. I never did know if Mrs. Nelson hired someone else. I was back to taking care of children and keeping house with Adeline. She played the piano, and I sang–maybe at church or something. Somewhere, somehow, we met Albert Buob. He was an excellent singer and liked to sing. He was taking care of a flock of sheep through the winter, and would stop in when he came to town for supplies. I went to Latah with him once in the spring. He had a car. (Short romance!)

Another farmer friend that I met there was Clarence Edgemond . I did not go out with him very much. I watched for his name in the paper to see who and when he married. He is probably dead like everybody else is by now. My favorite boyfriend was a schoolteacher from Blaine, Washington, Ted Bowen. I seemed to have a weakness for the name "Ted," beginning in high school.

While we were living here, Sherm, Adeline, and family and I went up the canyon to see the place where a large dam was intended to be constructed. Nothing particularly was memorable about it before the dam was built. Sherm Sterling must have been in Coulee for two years. In the spring of the second year, I got a job working in the United States Post Office. Mr. Edson, the postmaster, had a farm. Spring work was about to begin, which required more of his time. After I learned what I was supposed to do, he would be gone most of the day. It was interesting. I got acquainted with a lot more people that way. Once there was a letter addressed to "Onalaska, Washington." I had never heard of such a place. Where could it be? I looked it up in a directory so that I could send it in the right direction. I was paid $90 per month for that wonderful job. There were a lot of people who did not have a job at all, so that was real good.

When school was out in the spring, Sherm found out that his contract would not be renewed for the next year. He would have to find another school. They prepared to move back to his hometown, Kelso, Washington. What should I do? If I kept my job, I would have to pay board and room somewhere. I knew a good place, but would my job last, or was it only a "summer" job? Furthermore, I did not like to be totally separated from family, so in the end I moved to Kelso with them. (It was such a good job! Why didn't I stay there! I could have been there yet.)

Ruben Sterling, Sherm's father, came over with a big truck and helped them move. I might have expected him to look like an older version of Sherm–rather wiry, nervous, and bespectacled–instead he was a large, capable man with bright blue eyes.

Kelso was on the west side of the Cascade Mountains. It was quite a trip for him. They found a house in south Kelso for them to rent. I began looking for another job. Having worked in the post office I went there, but of course there was no employment there. Adeline and I soon found a full-gospel church that we could attend and where we could sing. I found a job as a domestic working in the home of Doctor A.F.V. (Arthur Franklin Vincent) Davis, and his wife, Elizabeth, where there was a small child to care for plus the usual chores. Finally Sherm got a job in Kettle Falls, Washington, and they moved away—leaving me alone in a strange land.

Part Two – Early Married Life
(1930's – 1940's)

—————————◆—◆—◆—————————

Kelso, Washington became my home. Sherm Sterling, Adeline, and family had moved again to Kettle Falls, to another school. I was employed by the Davis' in their home where my main job was child care.

Taking care of Arthur Junior, an only child about three years old was more than a challenge. He was adopted, as apparently Elizabeth Davis, the lady of the house, was barren. He was also a very much indulged child, who was locally famous in his own right. His presumed biological parentage was whispered. He had a play room with many toys. He was still quite small and slept in a crib in the room of his adopted parents.

There were two Davis brothers, who were both medical doctors and partners in practice together. Their office was a commercial building in the same block where the Pacific Highway (going north and south) intersected Allen Street, the main street of Kelso. It crossed the drawbridge over the Cowlitz River dividing the rowdier West Kelso from the more sedate (east) Kelso proper. Allen Street also divided Kelso. Allen Street and south were all flat lands in the Cowlitz, Columbia, and Coweeman River plains. From Allen Street north was the beginning of the hill on which Kelso clings–especially during high water. Because of the hill, these blocks were laid out without any alleys in the middle. Instead there was just a weed patch in the middle of the block. The office faced west to the Pacific Highway on its route between Allen Street and Academy Street. Three houses were built facing north on Academy Street.

The westernmost house on the intersection with the Pacific Highway was the residence of Dr. Arthur and Elizabeth Davis. The back door of the house was to the southeast and only a few steps from the back door of the office which was next door on Pacific. East of the house was a driveway where Dr. Arthur usually had his car parked rather than in the garage which was beyond it. Across the little strip of yard was the center house in the block which had been converted into a hospital–Kelso General Hospital. The easternmost house was that of Dr. Frank Davis, his wife, Mary, and their two little boys, Vincent and Brantley. Elizabeth and Mary Davis, although sisters-in-law living in such close proximity, would not speak to each other.

Dr. Frank paid me three dollars a month for sweeping out the office each morning. I soon familiarized myself with the routine, and felt quite comfortable there. My winter with Emelia and August prepared me for this. Mrs. Davis's cleaning regimen and demands were similar. She saw to it that I EARNED those five dollars a week. The first year I did have some evenings to myself. I got along fine with Arthur Junior, too. When I was alone doing some work, I sang a lot–as usual. A delivery man once came to the door and said, "Oh! I thought the singing was from the radio!" Mrs. Davis invited me to join her O.B. Choral Club, a group of singing girls who met up the street at the Kelso Methodist Church. She had parties for us along with our rehearsals. We all became good friends. We gave two concerts there at the church. Mrs. Davis liked to be conspicuously in the public eye, and to associate with the most prestigious people that she could find. At certain intervals, she entertained three tables for Bridge Parties. How beautifully we set the dining room table–for twelve–with the late refreshments. Her activities were usually written up in the local newspaper, *The Kelsonian*, a weekly publication printed by the County Commissioner at the time, George Umbaugh.

Before she left, Adeline and I found a full-gospel church, which we attended. Now I went alone. Ed Swanson was the pastor, and many of his relatives were members. I was very regular in my attendance. I had Thursday afternoons off, and sometimes I would go down to the Sterlings–I did some sewing there once.

As I mentioned, the McCabe family now lived in Portland, and Mr. McCabe was dead now. Jack and Vern lived with their mother. Jack worked for the Continental Can Company, and Vern worked as a policeman on a night shift. His mother worried a great deal about that. It was a dangerous occupation, and a hazardous time of day to be on his shift. One Sunday afternoon, Jack drove on the Pacific Highway to Kelso to see me. We went to a baseball game. I was not very interested in baseball, but it was nice to see Jack again. It was the last time I saw or heard of any of the McCabes for years.

I did a lot of embroidering, which was something that I could do for myself in the evenings. Later, my only escape from playing with Arthur Junior all evening was to go to church; and I did. At church, the Garrett family seemed interested in me. I joined them on several occasions–several girls and John. He followed the fruit harvest in Yakima and Wenatchee and must have been away a lot. I don't ever remember being alone with him.

The Davises often went on trips, so that Doctor could be away from the office on Sundays; and I was privileged to go along–that way I got acquainted with the surrounding area. One trip was outstanding! We went to Timberline Lodge on Mount Hood. It was built by WPA as a Federal project of the Great Depression. It is still a worthwhile place to visit. Another time, we spent a week at Seaside, Oregon, with the wife and children of another doctor. Doctor's niece, Kathryn Davis, must have been with us too. We donned bathing suits and went in water so cold, it made you numb. Once was enough, and I never did learn to swim. Kathryn became a dear friend, and with all of my friends at church, life was good.

One evening as I was walking down the street to church, who should come up beside me but Sherm's brother, "Chirp." What a surprise! (Once back in Coulee City Sherm had showed me a picture of his younger brother, and I had said to myself, "Ah! That's the man I hope to marry. But before I ever saw him in person, he was married to someone else.) At this time he was divorced from his wife and living with his folks at

~ 48 ~

210 Grade Street. He started to show up more frequently, but I never could persuade him to come in to church with me. One Thursday (my day off) I went to dinner with him. This was my chance to have some Cowlitz River Smelt, as Doctor did not care for the little fish. Chirp did not have a car, but sometimes he would borrow one from his friend (and former brother-in-law) Kenny Peterson. How did he know about John? He would ask me how I was getting along with the "Preacher Boy." Once we drove out to Coal Creek on the old, narrow road which avoided the lowlands and their inherent flooding by meandering along the adjoining flat, on a hill route. It seemed so far away.

Another time we went out the Coweeman River up in Rose Valley. We went fly fishing, brought the fish home to the Sterlings' house, and fried them. Where were his folks? Another day John stopped at Davises' to see me. I was working and couldn't ask him in or take time to visit. He simply announced that he wasn't seeing me any more. No regrets. I think he went to California. I do not know if he knew that I was seeing Chirp.

I went with the church group to a special meeting in Raymond, Washington, one Sunday, where I sang a number with Sarah Swanson accompanying me. It didn't work as well as with Adeline, and we didn't do it often. Singing with the Choral Club girls was best.

What did I know about economics? Or the Depression? Absolutely nothing! I didn't collect my wages regularly. I always kept track of how much money Doctor owed me, as he was my bank. I only asked him for money when I needed it to buy something personal–a coat or a dress– and that was not very often.

Chirp's mother called him "Theodore," and so, then, do I. He was working for the County Road District, probably because a family friend was the County Commissioner, George Umbaugh. His son, Dick, and Theodore grew up together. They both worked for the County. Theodore drove a gravel truck, maybe Dick did too. One week we planned that on my Thursday afternoon off, I would watch for his truck on the corner of the street where I lived, then I could spend the afternoon riding around with him. Even without a car, we managed to be together quite a bit. I thought that he was the most handsome, witty, and charming man that I ever met.

Week at Seaside, Oregon,
l-r Katherine Davis (Hall), RosaMae, Mrs. Davis

Week at Seaside, Oregon,
l-r Mrs. A.F.V. (Elisabeth) Davis, Charles, RosaMae

It was one evening in May when he brought me home to Davises' before we said goodbye that he asked me to marry him. I said, "Well, I'd think about it." I did think about it for days. This was a serious dilemma! I should not have allowed myself to ever be in love with a divorced man! Divorce was absolutely unacceptable in our family. Perhaps it would be best to just run away and forget him. So I wrote to "Mom" and told her that I would like to come back home for a while. I did not say why. She immediately wrote back saying, "No, no! Don't come home! No jobs here!" Well, what could I do? I wanted a home–somewhere. I decided that Theodore's divorce was HIS problem. He would probably marry somebody sometime, so it might as well be me.

Adeline and Sherm were in Kelso that summer for a visit. They planned to go back home to his school in Kettle Falls in August. It was a Sunday when I told Mrs. Davis that I wanted a day off on Monday in August. She protested, saying that there was washing to do. I insisted that the washing could wait, and that I would be there to take care of it the next day. So on Monday, August 1st, 1932, Theodore and I left Kelso with Sherm and Adeline. We stopped in Chehalis for a marriage license, then on to Tacoma. It was getting near five o'clock when we got there. Theodore was afraid the Courthouse would be closed if we didn't hurry, so he asked Sherm to let him drive. He did, and we made it in time. Sherm never could have done it. They were our witnesses, and then they dropped us off at the ferry dock, and continued their journey to Kettle Falls.

Now we were on our way to Bremerton where Florence (Sterling) and Pete Rasmussen were living at the time. Florence was an older sister of Theodore. I don't remember finding her, that day; but I remember that ferry ride across the water of Puget Sound. A Caribbean cruise could not have been more romantic! The setting sun was reflected beautifully in the water; and we were alone–together.

We found a bus that took us back to Kelso in time for us to be back to work the next morning. I liked the thought of being Mrs. T.H. Sterling. I'm sure I spent my Sundays with him after that. He had a room at his folks' place. Where would we live? There must have been much family discussion about this which I never heard. We couldn't live together very long in that one room.

LOCAL COUPLE WED IN TACOMA

Miss Rosa Mae Woodward Bride of Theodore Sterling

Miss Rosa Mae Woodward, of Kelso, daughter of Mr. and Mrs. O. C. Woodward, of Spokane, and Theodore Sterling, son of Mr. and Mrs. R. R. Sterling, of Kelso, were united in marriage in Tacoma Monday afternoon, his brother and sister-in-law, Mr. and Mrs. S R. Sterling of Kettle Falls, Wash., being the only witnesses to the ceremony performed in that city.

Miss Woodward is a popular member of Kelso's younger set and was a member of the O. B. Choral club, singing in the chorus and with the quartet of the group. She is a graduate of the Kelso high school in the class of 1928 and has made her home with Dr. and Mrs. A. F. V. Davis since her graduation.

The groom is employed by the county driving one of the county gravel trucks.

The marriage came as a complete surprise to their many friends here as they had not made their plans known, and it was a surprise when they returned from Tacoma where the ceremony was performed. Immediately following the wedding the young couple returned to their home here and Mr. and Mrs. S R. Sterling, who accompanied them to Tacoma, continued on their way to their home at Kettle Falls, after a visit here.

RosaMae Woodward Sterling,
August 1932

Theodore Henry Sterling,
August 1932

Reuben Sterling was a real farmer. His boys called him "Major." Rube, Dora, and their children Sherm, Florence, Esther, Theodore, and little Archie came west from Pennsylvania by train. They were on their way to Roseburg, Oregon, going south from Seattle with Simon, the brother of Rube, who was quite a rounder. He was the one who located their destination as Roseburg. They had been traveling for days, and nights, and days again. Florence and Esther had motion-sickness so badly and had vomited so much, they simply had to get off the train for a while. They disembarked at the Kelso Depot to have the earth under their feet again. There on the east bank of the Cowlitz River they walked across the flat to the Washington Hotel, where they checked in and stayed so that they could get their bowels together.

It was the spring of 1912 and smelt were "running" in the Cowlitz. The small fish were on their way from the Pacific to spawn in the fresh volcanic water of the Cowlitz River. Cowlitz Fish Company was processing them like mad. They were for sale for a penny a bucket–any sized bucket. Rube was so impressed, that he looked around and decided to stay. Simon ("That dirty Sime," as Dora referred to him for the rest of her life) seems to have disappeared about this time. Rube cashed in their tickets and stayed in Kelso.

By now, the Sterlings lost most everything that they had accumulated, due to the Great Depression. Their lands and houses were now gone; and quite humbled, they decided to move to a farm in Chehalis, Washington, leaving their misfortunes behind them. Theodore could have the Grade Street house if he would pay off the mortgage. I don't know how much that was, but it was certainly good for us. I stayed with my job at Davises'. By this time they were my "family." She and the Choral Club girls gave me a bridal shower. She had difficulty finding my replacement. I think that it was October when I finally left the Davis house and moved into our house. We had to buy a kitchen range to cook on, a table and four chairs, and a heater on the time-payment plan.

Theodore had a rug and some living room furniture left over from his previous marriage. Florence's piano was left in the house as well as Esther's sewing machine. I was so glad to have them both! I learned to sew, and I played piano by the hour. I certainly enjoyed my new home!

I still helped Mrs. Davis some. Once she told me she had a problem with the new girl's washing. Arthur Junior's clothes were just rotting away. "Oh," I told her, "she's using too much Clorox and not washing it out of the material." Another time she asked me to wash and iron her big beautiful (and expensive) tablecloth. And, of course, Arthur Junior would also come to spend time with me frequently.

I wonder if we had Thanksgiving in Chehalis? Maybe not, without a car. Food was cheap, but so were wages. Theodore made about seventy dollars per month. After we made payments on the mortgage, the furniture, and utilities, we were lucky to have ten dollars left to buy groceries. So, I watched for sales as much as possible. Two dozen eggs sold for twenty-five cents; pork, ten cents a pound; other things were priced proportionately. We decided that we needed a garden in our back yard the very next spring.

Christmas came and somehow we got a duck to roast. That was different. I am sure that I fixed other appropriate things even though we did not plan to have company. While I was cooking Theodore said, "I think I'll go over to Moores' for a while." I was busy and didn't mind. Theodore's younger brother, Archie, was married to Mary Moore. Mary had several brothers and maybe a sister still at home. I'd never met them. After a few hours, however, dinner must have been ready. Theodore came home–drunk as could be. That certainly was a new experience for me. I had never been around anyone like that before. He was never abusive; just disgustingly stupid. He either sat or lay on the davenport all afternoon. Every time I looked at him I would burst into tears, so I must have just put the food away. Late in the afternoon, Bob Rasmussen, the younger brother of Florence's husband, Pete, stopped in. I was certainly embarrassed to have him find us in such a situation. My eyes and nose were red from crying.

I knew that Theodore had a bottle hidden away in the closet–since Prohibition was still in force–so he could take a little "snort" occasionally. That seemed okay to me, but drunkenness made him totally repulsive to me. Then I began to resent that bottle and hide it or get rid of it. One time I especially remember a time when he came home from work dirty and drunk. I tried to give him a bath and clean him up before he went to bed. It didn't work. After I cleaned the bowel movement out of the bathtub it was the last time I ever did that. Fortunately his drinking did not happen very often. Back to normal when winter came, it became evident that a baby was on the way. In the spring, I wanted Theodore to come with me to visit my folks. I wanted to show off my handsome husband to family and friends. We could use the money that doctor still owed me for the trip, so we did. He enjoyed shooting squirrels on the farm, where the folks must have still been living at that time.

Spring came. We must have planted the garden as planned. Neither of us had experience with gardening. It was just a good idea to try. In June, the run-off water from the heavy melting snows caused the Columbia River to rise. The dike broke and all of south Kelso was flooded. There was extra work for the County Crew. They helped people move to higher ground. Across the street from our house there on Grade Street, was a bakery and a dwelling in several feet of water. It took quite a while for that water to disappear.

I could use a little extra money to accumulate the necessities for the new baby that was due in September. I was rather hoping for a boy, since there had been so many girls in our family. Dick Umbaugh's wife, Cleo, was also expecting, so I made a baby thing for her, too. I think that our baby came first; it was on the thirteenth of September, 1933. I went to Kelso General Hospital, where Dr. Davis took care of me and our much-loved baby girl was born. I was sure that she would have dark hair like her parents and I remembered the Oley Speaks song:

Sylvia's hair is like the night,
Touched with glancing, starry beams –
Such a face as drifts through dreams
This is Sylvia to the sight.
And the touch of Sylvia's hand
Is as light as milkweed down
When the leaves are gold and brown
And the autumn fills the land.

That is how she happened to be called "Sylvia;" her middle name,

Ann, was for my mother.

As was customary, I must have had some help when I first came home from the hospital. That may be how I met Olive Coleman, a young Salvation Army lass, and dear person to become our friend forever. We bought a baby buggy so that I could wheel baby with me up town to pay bills and buy groceries.

Another Thanksgiving came and went. In December Kelso had another disaster. This time the Cowlitz River flooded. It washed away a whole farm near Castle Rock. Theodore saw the chicken house hit the Allen Street Bridge. Chickens flew everywhere. Other trash was piling up dangerously on the piers of the bridge and starting to form a dam. The lowlands north of the hill in north Kelso were flooded. The County Crew was working overtime again. It must have been in the late afternoon that day when the Coweeman dike broke and the floodwater began pouring in on our side of Grade Street. I listened to empty fruit jars and firewood bumping around afloat in our basement as the water rose. By midnight the water had risen to the top step. Mercifully, it halted there. Our floors were dry. I'm not sure how late the County Crew worked that night–hauling gravel to try to stop that breach in the dike. Next morning Doctor Davis came down to take me home, and found that I was all right and that I did not need to go. All of our neighbors on Vine Street were in deep water–as was our old garage and garden spot. Eventually the water subsided as it did in the spring flood. What a mess!

Theodore was an outdoor-type of person. His public education stopped at grade eight. When he was a very young man, he spent a lot of time living with Bert Middleton, a bachelor, in the upper Coweeman River area where they were tending dam. Those were the days when the logging companies would roll their branded logs down to the river, and when all was ready, open the flood gates of the dam so that the water would wash their logs down to the Columbia River and to market. Roads were too impassable. It took days with teams of horses and wagons to take supplies to the logging camps. Theodore and Bert lived off the land as much as possible by hunting and fishing, but they had to hike to town or to a half-way point called the White House, for basic supplies. During these years he became acquainted living in the area now called Rose

Valley. Those days, it was called Shanghai.

Mert Curry lived there with his mother on the family farm. He also worked for the County and drove by our house every day on the way to work at the County Shop in West Kelso, so Theodore rode to work with him. Other upper Coweeman friends were McDonalds, Jabushes, Nesbitts, Old Blackey, Jake and Katherine Nordvick, Edgie Toehill, Herb Middleton, and more. They belong in his autobiography rather than mine.

One day Theodore did not come home with Mert as usual, but arrived in a model T Ford that he bought for twenty dollars. I wondered how we could spare that much money. I was pleased that we could now drive out to Archie's or go pick blackberries along the roads. I don't remember going out of Cowlitz County. Once we were as far as Castle Rock when something went wrong. Baby Sylvia was with us. I do not remember how we got home; but it did ruin our day.

Another holiday season went by. Did we go to Chehalis? Yes, it seems so; but I don't remember how we got there or got back home. I decided that we would always spend Christmas at home when Sylvia was older. The following summer we were invited to go on a camping trip on the Klickitat River with Ralph and Vivian Goodrich. Ralph also worked for the County Road Crew. They had a little boy not much older than Sylvia. On the way, they stopped at Davis Terraces where Dick and Cleo Umbaugh lived. They persuaded them to join us. That was really too many. Imagine two little kids and six grown-ups in the car on a hot day. The men stopped at a beer joint for refreshments while we waited in the car with two thirsty little kids. When we finally arrived at the river, it was a lovely place. Probably the reason that I found that such a miserable trip was because I was just beginning a new pregnancy.

Time passed uneventfully through the fall and winter except that my sister, Lillian came during that time. There was a heavy run of smelt that spring. We drove up the Cowlitz River to Sandy Bend one day in early March, went down to the river and found a school of smelt going by right close to the shore. She stepped on a log in the river so that she could reach down into the water and scoop out some fish. Then the log began to move. She got some fish; but she also got wet.

The last week in March Archie was taken to the hospital seriously ill with a burst appendix. His mother came down to Kelso again to stay with us through this ordeal. The evening of April 1st I said, "I'm going to the hospital, too." Our baby was not due for another week or so, and they thought I was just playing an April Fool joke on them at first. I was taken to the Longview Hospital (St. Johns or Cowlitz General) this time because the County had some kind of medical and health benefits through it to their employees.

There was our healthy baby boy. How we happened to choose "Maurice" for his name is a mystery. Maybe it should have been "Orace" like my father. (We did pronounce it "Morris.") It was Lillian who took care of things at home while I was in the hospital, and when I first came back home. All went well. I took lots of pictures of our babies. Sometime later she found a job working for the Colemans, who had a hardware store in town. Much like mine, they had a baby boy and the housekeeping to take care of; but Mrs. Coleman spent some of her time at their store.

We seemed to be prospering financially. Theodore got a higher-paying job running the road-grader like Mert. Roads were all gravel instead of being paved like they are now. We must have paid off our debt for the furniture. When I made the last payment on the mortgage, the man complimented me for not missing a single payment. He wished all of his customers were like that. Sometime in here Theodore got a better car.

It must have been the following spring, when tax time came around, that we found out that the taxes were delinquent and that our place would be sold for back taxes. I never did know how much money was involved. Theodore was angry and disappointed; and wouldn't pay the taxes at all. The neighbor across the street bought the place, and then tried to persuade Theodore to redeem it, saying it was well worth it and he still had the right to recover it. But Theodore was done with it and began looking for another place for us to live.

He found one down by the Cowlitz River where we could have a big garden in the sandy soil and keep a cow. We had to borrow a few hundred dollars for all this. The house was just awful. It was single-wall construction, so there was no sign of insulation at all; just one board separated inside from outside. The kitchen sink drained through a hole in the floor onto the ground immediately under the house. He had to dig a septic tank for that. There was no other plumbing at all. He put flooring down in the large front room. There were two small bedrooms off of the living room. We glued heavy felt-paper to the bedroom walls and ceilings to keep out the cold. We gave our nicest rug to Archie and Mary, and maybe other things as well. We were finally fitted comfortably (?) into this smaller house–piano, sewing machine, and all. No more use for the baby buggy; it was too far from town now to walk there to pay bills or buy groceries.

We built a small chicken house, hoping to sells eggs like his father was doing in Chehalis. For some reason our chickens were not as productive. They did lay just enough eggs to pay the chicken-feed bill. One evening Lillian came over to stay with the children so that I could go to a Choral Club party at Mrs. Davis'. I put Maurice to bed as usual, thinking that he would never know that I was gone at all. Wrong! When I got home, the poor little tyke was standing limply in the corner of his crib STILL sobbing. Neither Lillian nor Theodore could comfort him. He was such a "mamma's boy"! He learned to walk there. We had a nice back yard where he could play, and I tied him loosely to the clothes line so that he could go the full length and width. That didn't work; he wasn't happy there. There was no fence in the front of the house to keep the children out of the road; but there was very little traffic.

Yes, Arthur Junior even came to visit here occasionally. Also while we were living here my other sister, Lucille, came over from eastern Washington with her fiance, Jack Hafstad. He was a Scandinavian who spoke Swedish and English. They were married in the Longview Foursquare Church. Sylvia was the flower girl for the occasion. We tried to make it as festive as possible. Lillian married the next year. I do not remember any wedding. Johnny Weiler, her husband, was the youngest of three Weiler brothers all of whom were gifted mechanics. Each one of us Woodward sisters married men who had been married before.

Theodore and I had aimed at being as self-sufficient as possible there in the house by the river; and we were. He raised several calves and then finished them for market up at Archie's place at Carrolls. We paid off all of our debts, and probably had a better car to show for it. We made trips to Chehalis to see his folks. He wanted more space, like Mert Curry had up in Rose Valley, or even like Archie. He inquired about a place advertised by a real estate company. It was located out in the Coal Creek area.

When he discussed this with his father, Rube discouraged him saying that hill land was not very good for farming. Theodore took me out to look at the place, and I thought that it was wonderful. All those bare hills were just like the Palouse Hills that were a part of my youth. What a lovely little stream with all that interesting vegetation along the road–just like the Girl of the Limberlost. O! I was so afraid that he wouldn't buy it; but he did. The value of our property there by the river was enough to cover the down payment. There was 569 acres of contiguous property. Now we owed the Federal Land Bank $5,000 additional dollars. I was delighted, and singing Cole Porter's

Just give me land, lots of land
'Neath the starry skies above.
DON'T FENCE ME IN.

Someone had the place rented. A man was living there to take care of a flock of sheep. It was February of 1939 before we could move in. The County road ended about half a mile from the house. The rest of the way up the muddy canyon we were on our own.

Theodore hired a neighbor to move our household goods with a team of horses and a wagon–and they got everything including the piano. We had supper in town that night, then drove out there, parked, and walked up that dark route with a flash light and anything else we could carry with two rather frightened and reluctant children. When we arrived at our destination, there was a small kerosene lamp to light our way to bed. Did we have the beds set up first? I don't remember; but the lamp cast shadows that folks with electricity don't know about. My grandpa Pittman used to entertain us children by making shadow pictures on the wall with his hands...rabbits, birds, etc.

Next day we could explore our new world in the daylight. We lived in one big room at the east end of the house, and another small adjoining room for a bedroom. The roof leaked in one spot there. The rest of the house-dining room, kitchen, and another bedroom, needed more repairs. Also adjoining the kitchen was a pantry. Beyond the kitchen door outside was a well-insulated cooler (room). In its day it had been a wonderfully efficient device. Water from the spring, a constant flow, was the cooling source.

West of the house was a stream of water coming down the hill. That was the source of our water supply. The Stewarts had spent a lot of money on that place—a well-built house (with plumbing), a Delco lighting system (electricity), a large barn, and then stumped the entire largest piece of the most level land so that they could raise hay.

The barn had been burned down probably by hunters. Every fixture in the house was gone, stolen. The neighbor who moved us never would haul any firewood to our house, so Theodore had to carry a day's supply from the car to the house every day until the road was dry in the spring. There was such an overwhelming amount of work to be done! Archie helped put cedar shakes on the roof, and maybe other things, too. The west end of the house had to be jacked up, leveled, and supported by a new foundation. Then we could replace the windows which had been shot out, and use the rest of the house. It had been constructed as a bunkhouse for the loggers to clear the old-growth forest. The site was selected because the water source was near, of sufficient altitude above the building, constant, and excellent in every way.

The road had to be finished and constructed to connect the house to Stewart Creek Road and the County network before another winter. Somehow it all got done. Theodore hired his friends, the County Road Crew, to haul gravel on our road one Saturday—their day off. He and Mert Curry had our cleared land cultivated and planted to oats. It was not very good hay. Too much bracken fern grew up in it; but they had another patch of ground for hay down in Longview. So finally we had a place for our cows just like Mert. We also had a big garden spot. Gradually things improved. We took the wall out between one bedroom and the dining room making it into one big living-dining room. We could use the kitchen and pantry. Actually, we ate at our kitchen table unless we had company. Sylvia's bedroom was off the kitchen. I painted all the 4-inch select tongue-in-groove interior lumber with white paint. With two Aladdin lamps it seemed quite bright, cheerful, and spacious.

That first September Sylvia would be six years old, and it would be time for her to go to public school. I felt real sad to have her go and to have to share her with someone else. It was a mile from our house to the Coal Creek Store, where she would catch the school bus. I thought it was too far for her to walk alone. We arranged for her to attend the Catlin School in West Kelso rather than attending Longview schools. She would go to work with her dad and stay with Mrs. Curry, who lived near the County Shop and the school. Then Sylvia could walk to school and back to Mrs. Curry's to come home with him again. Mert's mother moved to this place in town after Mert married Ethel Jabush, a widowed neighbor.

One Christmas my folks sent us a battery operated radio. It was a real treat! I listened to soap operas: *The Guiding Light, Stella Dallas,* etc. Maurice liked *The Lone Ranger*. There was quite a bit of space between the wall and the wood-burning kitchen range. Often he would play there in the warm space with his toys. Sometimes he would fall asleep there too and take a little nap there on the imitation-tile linoleum. I did not see as much of Lillian any more since she finished her job at Coleman's and got married. We lived quite a good distance apart from each other now.

One pleasant summer day we had visitors from Clark Creek, John and Sadie Watson. Their land joined us on the southeast. It was a hillside we could see from our house on the opposite hill. She remembered visiting the Stewarts when they were living in our house. How nice it was! The Nelsons, who lived at the end of Clark Creek Road, also walked over to visit once. I learned that their daughter once worked for Mrs. Davis too. Our nearest neighbors down our road, were the Lane family, Ed, Opha, and their children, Norma, Betty, and Bob; then across from them was the Heitz family, then down across the road again was old Mr. Ackers, then Booths, and McCaslands, and across Coal Creek Road was the Coal Creek Store. They were such pleasant neighbors– all of them. Farther up the Coal Creek Road and across the creek was Antilla's Dairy. They used to pasture their cows on the Stewart place before the barn was destroyed.

Beyond their place was the Bob Carlon farm. Bob Carlon had a small herd of cattle that went wild. He never could get them home; and they would show up at our place every once in a while. We didn't want our "Daisy" to join up with them. Bob told Theodore to shoot them and let him know so that he could call the slaughter-house in Kelso and they could come and get the carcasses for meat. So, over a period of time, one by one they disappeared, until one lonely little calf came home with our cows and lived with them. Yes, we had our stump-ranch just like Mert. Dad Sterling gave Theodore four nice Holstein heifers. We only milked our "Daisy," up in a shed the renters had used.

I think that Sylvia and Maurice enjoyed the summer. Maurice caught his first fish on a bent pin on a string with a worm. It was a mud-dauber. He was so proud of it! I guess that pretty much got him hooked on fishing. We also had a little pig that he befriended. That pig would follow Daisy, the cow, out to pasture. When she came home to lie down under the apple tree, the pig would lie down right against her back. I am sure that the summer passed pleasantly. I don't know just when Theodore quit working for the county. He and Archie began a logging project on the Wages place in the Elochoman River Valley near Cathlamet, in the next County west (Wahkiakum). Theodore bought a crawler tractor, and with it he was to provide logs for Archie's saw mill. Theodore was a good logger. They finally gave up the sawmill and just did logging.

Lillian was living at Sandy Bend now on a little farm in a house that looked east over the Cowlitz River. It had two bedrooms upstairs, and one down. There was no way that I could help her when her baby boy, Jerry, was born in May of 1941. She was so good to me; and I could not return the favor. I was too far away. I, too, had a baby on the way; and my babies were most welcome. September came. By this time Sylvia and Maurice were going to Longview schools. I baked a nice cake for her eighth birthday on September 13th and took pictures as we always did on birthdays. Unfortunately my abdomen protruded a lot because this baby was going more on ten months than nine. I brushed the frosting off of her cake, so had to turn the cake around for pictures. Nobody ever let me forget it. The next day I knew my baby would be coming. I didn't mention it to Theodore because I was sure he would be coming home from work in time, even though Cathlamet was quite a distance away.

Evening and suppertime came and went, and he still did not come home. What was I to do? There was no telephone. I just waited. When twelve o'clock midnight came, I said to myself, if he is not here in 30 minutes, I must walk down to Lanes and have someone take me to the hospital. He did get home just barely in time, and took me to Dr. Davis's Kelso General Hospital, where baby came into our world about six o'clock in the morning. While I was there for the usual week or so, Bertha-May Stanley stayed at our house and took care of things. She was a relative of Lillian's best friends, the Bean family. We met at church.

In December of that year, I heard on the radio about the bombing of Pearl Harbor and the beginning of World War II. When I was a little girl and World War I was going on, I thought that war was a constant state, because I could not remember a time when it was not going on. Now I could see another one staring the world in the face. Theodore was thirty eight years old, and would be thirty nine in April. Would he be drafted into the army?

Maybe they were through logging on the Wages place when Archie and Theodore decided to set up the shingle mill on Hay Mountain, where there was an abundance of excellent cedar available. It was a long way back and forth to work. Theodore met two brothers who had property nearby. One of the men had a job in Longview and was driving back and forth each day. So he and Theodore decided to exchange dwellings temporarily, so that each of them would be closer to their work. Maybe it was October when we moved to Hay Mountain. Sylvia went to school on the bus with the neighbor boy, to Cathlamet. There was a shed there for Daisy, our cow. I don't remember what arrangement was made for our other cows on the farm. The house we moved into was much like our house down by the river. Again we were in single-wall construction without a shred of insulation. It seemed unusual that there was electricity there–so far out in the country. I could use my electric washing machine. Water was the problem. We had to haul water to drink, and use the water caught in the barrel off of the roof for everything else. It rains so much that time of year, there was enough water.

The wind blew constantly. Trees up there are one-sided. One particularly cold day Theodore stayed home from work to nail cardboard onto the walls to help keep out the cold. I sat by the stove to nurse the baby. I was too warm on the stove side, and too cold on the other side. Maurice was playing on the floor nearby. I made him go to bed for a while–just to get warm. My neighbor taught me to knit. She kept her family in sweaters. I used her basic pattern and made one for Maurice. That maroon sweater was his favorite. When the elbows wore out, I knitted new sleeve ends; but finally he out-grew it. I tried planting a garden there in the spring. Nothing grew. I could see that was why the fruit trees that were planted there did not grow. NOTHING GREW. With summer came drier weather. There was not so much water from the roof. How I wished that we were back at OUR home, where we had plenty of wonderful water. Summer would be difficult here, if not impossible, with diapers to wash.

Lillian and Johnny and their little Jerry came clear up on Hay Mountain to see us once before I went to Latah with the children in June. At Latah I asked "Mom" if I could please stay with them through the summer until we could move back to our house on Coal Creek again. I got the same answer that I had gotten years before. "No, no! You can't stay here!" My dear Bob came to the rescue. I stayed in his house, next door to "Mom" in Latah, while his family stayed on the farm where he was working. I did their washing, kept the house in town, and occasionally cooked for his hired men when they were working near the town of Latah.

It may have been about the middle of July when Theodore had an accident. He was filing a large, circular saw at the mill, when his foot slipped and he fell into the saw still with the file between his hands. The large saw teeth stabbed him under his arm as his arm caught his weight. He drove himself to Cathlamet where Dr. Fritz had his office, to stop the gusher of blood. Dr. Fritz said that he was very lucky. The saw teeth had gone on either side of the artery. Had the artery been cut, he would not have made it to town. He could not work for a while, and I wanted him to come over and spend the recovery time with me in Latah, but he wouldn't. Finally, sometime in August, I was happy to move back to our home again.

By now Theodore was wondering if he would be drafted into military service. At 39, he was at a borderline age. He, Dick Umbaugh, and Ralph Goodrich all joined the Army Engineers Corps. Those weeks before he left (which was sometime in October) were spent in preparation. He bought a better used car. I had to learn how to drive it. He sold all the cows except Daisy and another heifer that I could take care of in the small barn up by the house. He put in and stored a winter's supply of firewood in the woodshed. Dad Sterling built a garage for the car out of shakes and poles, and scraps. It was a very sturdy building. We had a few chickens in another small shed of a chicken coop. We must have had canned stuff. I dreaded driving the car, and went to town only about twice a month. "Practice makes perfect," they say, so I must have gained confidence in my driving so I could go to the Coal Creek Church. Preparation time ended when Theodore went off to Panama.

We were well prepared for winter. The necessary things had all been done and we were home with plenty of water, food, firewood, and all. Sylvia and Maurice walked down the road to catch the school bus at the Coal Creek Store, as they both attended Longview schools. They caught the same bus at the same time, and walked together both ways. One day in winter the school closed early because of a severe snow storm. It was a blizzard. My two little ones would have to walk a mile home in that awful storm. There was no way for me to help them, as I could not leave the baby all alone in the house. I just paced the floor, kept the fires going in both stoves, paced the floor, and watched out the window to the road down the hill to searching for two small figures that finally appeared trudging up the hill to the house. When they arrived, Maurice's pant-legs were frozen stiff; he was crying, and cold. Sylvia said, "I told him to walk in my tracks, but he wouldn't do it."

Spring came as usual with nicer weather. Baby had learned to walk. He wanted to come out in the yard with me when I hung up the laundry that I had hand-washed onto the clotheslines. The dog that we had then would growl at him threateningly. I did not think that the baby was safe around that dog. It was late March when Daisy was due to freshen when she failed to come home one evening. I couldn't leave long to go and look for her. I must have been milking the other cow.

Theodore turned 40 in the middle of April, and he came back home again. He was faithful to send home his checks, and wrote about his adventures in Panama. He was desperately ill once and had difficulty finding help. In all the time he was gone, none of the Sterlings ever contacted me to see how I was doing. We found out that Archie and Mary got a divorce that winter. When the payment was due on the place that spring, we had saved enough money to pay it off, even though the shingle mill venture had failed. Theodore went to work now for a logging company. Later, after Archie was married to Ina, he and Archie began "gyppo" logging on their own with each other.

My contact with the Davises diminished. I do remember vaguely spending a night or a long evening at Davises' with Baby. It might have been so that I could be with the Choral Club girls. Of course, I did stop in briefly a few times. It was sometime in the 1940's that Mrs. Davis was having severe asthma attacks. Doctor thought that a drier climate would give her relief. I do not know where she went, but she died there–alone. Doctor felt terrible. Soon his health began to fail. His niece, Kathryn, came from California to stay with him. I stayed with him one day, myself.

He asked me to cook some chicken and dumplings for him. He was in bed. We visited. What words of encouragement could I possibly give him? He was sort of like my father. That was the last time I saw him. He moved to California and lived with Kathryn the rest of his life, died, and was buried there. Kathryn and I always kept in touch with each other.

Part Three – Middle Married Life
(1950's – 1960's)

Theodore and Archie worked well together. They enjoyed each other and their work. They were also successful. Apparently, Ina, Archie's new wife who must have been doing the bookkeeping, was dissatisfied with how the profit was shared, so they split up. Archie went to work for Weyerhaeuser, and Theodore hired Verle Flatt to work for him in the woods. Work on our farm never ceased. We got cows again. Theodore must have taken over the milking again. I remember a roan-colored cow that he didn't like very well. He hoped to replace her with another that would freshen in the fall. When the replacement cow was due, she disappeared. When he found her she was dead–probably milk fever– but there was a hungry little calf near her. Another nice, big Holstein heifer did the same thing. We never did find her. I told Theodore that we needed a fenced barnyard to keep them in when they were due.

We decided to try sheep, and traded some cows and bought a flock late in the summer. I don't remember how many we had. I just remember using the barn down the hill for the sheep now. We started with Romney, a dual-purpose breed. They did not seem to require much hay. That thick coat of wool covered their skinny bodies. They went out to pasture every day, and came back home every night. The lamb crop was poor because the ewes were thin. We met Sheldon McFadden and his old bachelor uncle, Louie Tooker, who tended his sheep and lived alone with them way back off Coal Creek Road, and did not even have a road to his place. Louie was a mustard gas victim in World War I, and spent the rest of his life mentally challenged. He was odd, dirty, and rather harmless. He would stop at the Coal Creek Store and buy Twinkies which he seemed to get on himself, much to the fascination of the local kids who did not know quite what to make of him. He would walk to Kelso and get drunk, so there was no telling where or when he would show up–often with a bottle of vanilla extract in his pocket for alcohol.

Sheldon sheared our sheep every spring. There was no electricity, so he had a very noisy generator that frightened all the sheep. It was hard work, but he got the job done. He also helped me clean the barn, was a good friend, and advised us on sheep as well as our gardening activities. His wife, Emma, was a cook at the Elks Lodge I think. They had children, a boy about Sylvia's age, and a couple of older girls. Later in the new barn with electricity available, his relative, Jim Newman always sheared our sheep. He still has sheep of his own that he shows at Fairs. After Louie died and the road got put in, they built a house on the property which was then called Woodside Drive. When Emma was widowed and alone, Theodore took care of her bees for her.

Especially in the spring, when lambs were imminent, we put the sheep in the yard in case of predators. Sometimes sheep get caught by their wool in the heavy canes full of thorns of blackberry bushes, so we had to count them every evening at feeding time to be sure that they were all there. We had bells on some of them. There was a fence around the yard of our house to keep the cows away. One moonlit night after we went to bed, the dog began to bark. The bells on the sheep were ringing as they ran. We looked out of our bedroom door that was open for air, and we saw a huge bear coming toward us up the hill. Theodore quickly got his gun off of its mounted deer-head, with antler gun rack, and shot the bear. It ran down the hill and through the fence with the dog following all the way. Theodore dressed quickly and followed the dog to see if the bear was down. This was the first time we had bear meat. The kids took bear meat sandwiches to school, and the other kids talked about it; and we got a reputation for having bears in the woods.

The next time we got a bear it was in the late afternoon. Theodore was taking a nap, I was cooking dinner, and the boys were outside playing ball. They saw the bear and woke up their dad. It was east of the house on its way down the hill. He shot it and it rolled down to the bottom of the hill, which was hundreds of feet. Theodore and the dog were right behind it. Sylvia was talking to her boyfriend on the telephone and told what was going on. They went to the Coal Creek Store and told them what was going on at our house. Glen Schweikhardt at the store stood out in the middle of Coal Creek Road and told every car that Chirp Sterling just shot a bear and was dressing it out and directed them right up little Stewart Creek Road.

Soon all the men coming home from work that stopped at the store, were on their way up the road to see the bear. Families came and trooped over there where Ray Steinauer was helping cut it all up and distributing it to all comers. Cars were parked everywhere. It was a big traffic jam. Theodore was a famous man in the neighborhood now. Since it was in the early fall, the bear meet tasted good. We used it just like Bert Middleton, but we didn't get much of this bear. It was all carried away piece by piece. Even the teeth and claws were taken. Only the entrails remained as coyote food. Theodore told the kids not to talk about it if he shot another bear. We did not have enough left to even take much to Bert.

One spring in March when we were still living in the old house, our neighbors, the Lanes were coming up to spend the evening with us. They had a camera which took slide pictures that we watched on a movie screen at their house, or a little viewer at ours. As yet Chuck Booth had not wired the old house, and we did not have a line extended beyond Lane's house. They had beautiful flowers, and a nice garden. They photographed various flowers up close, and they were lovely pictures. They also photographed their travels, and what caught their eye in the neighborhood. I wanted to get the chores done and dinner over with as soon as possible. I put a casserole in the oven and thought that I could speed things up a bit if I went after the cow myself instead of sending Maurice. I could hear the bell on the hill across the creek. I've chased cows home before, and when you get them started toward home, it is best just to follow because they know the best paths.

It did not work with this cow. I realized that she was not going home when I look around and nothing looked familiar. Then I couldn't figure out which direction was home. I was really lost. It was getting dark. I thought I'd have to stay there all night. In the morning I could climb down into the canyon and see which way the water was running and follow it out. What a miserable inconvenience! I don't know what prompted me to yell a loud YOO-HOO. I chided myself because I thought that no one could hear me and there was no use yelling my guts out. Then I heard something; so I tried it again. Sure enough there was a reply coming closer and closer. It was Theodore and Maurice. They said that we were nearer to Clark Creek so we'll go out that way. So we soon arrived in someone's back yard MUCH to their surprise. They drove us around on the roads to our place in their car to where our guests were still waiting with our youngest boy, Ted. It was about nine o'clock. What an evening! The casserole? I'm pretty sure the fire went out, and we visited with the Lanes another time.

Now that I could drive the car, I began to go regularly to the Coal Creek Church nearby. It was built as a small school building, and now functioned as a church. We hardly ever had a preacher, but we kept the Sunday school going for the many local children. I taught nearly every class at one time or another. There were never enough teachers. I once invited a neighbor to bring her children to Sunday school and the day she came, the teacher for that class was absent. Since I had yet another class on my hands, I just gave her the material and asked her to take the class that was mainly her own two children. I was embarrassed. She never came back to church again. I was the secretary, and ordered Sunday school material. Our funds were desperately limited. On the seventy-fifth anniversary of the church, a detailed history was written from its beginning right up to date. Now the building is much improved, it has a parsonage, and a paid pastor, and indoor plumbing in the basement.

I'll just remember a Christmas program that we did once with a tree, the nativity scene, and all. It was very well-attended. Mr. Lane bribed Ted to sing for us:

Jolly old Saint Nicholas

Lean your ear this way.
Don't you tell a single soul
What I'm going to say, etc.

He was about four years old. Just down and across the creek from the church was Bob Carlon's farm. He sold or rented it to a family with three children who were about the same age as mine were at the time. She helped in the church a lot. Bob Carlon built another house for himself close to the store and it was later occupied by the Bob Richards family.

I have said it before. I will say it again. Theodore was a good logger. He learned how to run property lines with a compass, and did a lot of it. He always wanted to be sure of the property lines so that he did not cut someone else's timber by accident. He would find property corners and boundaries, at the places where he logged as well as at home. He also learned how to cruise timber accurately. Often it meant borrowing time on the Coal Creek Store adding machine during after-hours. This way he knew what the market value of the timber that he was bidding on was actually worth, how much of each species there was, and with his experience with heavy equipment, he could also estimate the cost of building the necessary roads. He was an artist as a cat-skinner, or operating the crane, grader, shovel, or any piece of heavy equipment. He also earned a reputation for being able to fell a tree accurately. A man who had a business at Oak Point asked him to come down there and look at a tree that would have to be felled between two buildings. Could he? Would he do it? It was close quarters, but he did it. He was a very careful in his work. There was never a threat of legal action from anyone.

It must have been the first year or so that somehow we acquired two geese and a gander. I know that Maurice was a little boy, and that gander would attack him dangerously if he happened to come too close to the little barn where we kept the milk-cow. The goose had a nest under there; another goose had a nest farther away. When they both hatched all their eggs, we had quite a flock of geese for the holiday market. We put an ad in the paper. We killed, scalded, and plucked the feathers off those geese, and delivered them to our customers. I saved that wonderful goose down and feathers for pillows. It was okay once, but too much work to go through all that again. We often had several more as pets, and we ate the eggs instead of hatching them.

Theodore did take time from his logging to plow up a patch of land for a garden. I could help quite a bit with that. There were other improvements. I think that it was the winter that Theodore was in Panama that Lillian's husband, Johnny installed a sink in the kitchen so that I didn't have to carry all the waste water out to dump it. This was a real blessing. Later improvements were accomplished, but I don't know what years. Another year Theodore built a large concrete holding tank for the water from the spring so that we could have it on a gravity demand system. We always had wonderful water–even in the driest season. Then he cleared the line right-of-way for a PUD electric utility line to come up the road from Lane's house to ours, put in the poles so that we got electricity and a telephone to the Stewart house. This meant a refrigerator at last. We always had a cold storage locker rented with our goods in it, so we were used to it that way.

One summer he brought his "cat" home and put a dam with a concrete spillway across Stewart Creek, cleaned out all the vegetation that rising water would submerge, and made a big pond over a swampy spot. Maurice took a fishing pole and a bucket, caught little trout, and dumped them into the pond so that it would be stocked with cut-throats–Theodore's favorite fish. This took a lot of little fishing trips and buckets carried home. The geese loved the new accommodations as much as the little trout. The fish seemed to grow to proportionate size with their large, new home in the pond. Twelve to fourteen inches was about average. The biggest caught that we knew of was 16 inches. He put in a few bullfrogs too, while he was at it. They tried to reproduce, but the winters were too cold, I guess, and big masses of tadpoles failed to over-winter. Finally the frogs got old and quit trying to reproduce. They live quite a while. Theodore's sister, Esther, laughed and nick-named it the "Frog Farm."

Finally, as we were prospering, I said that it was time to have a larger house-with three bedrooms. I wondered if I should look for a house in town. "No," he said; "We'll build it right here." So I looked at house plans that winter, and decided that I really didn't know anything about houses. Maybe an architect would advise me. No, they don't. Much later, our builders, Govert and Henry Swanson said that there was no such thing as a perfect house plan. There's always something that you wish was different. They should know, having built many houses in Kelso (including the one Archie and Ina were living in). These were nephews of Ed Swanson. They had built a big, new church where the families continued to worship. They converted what had been the Swanson farm, into the Swanson Addition to Kelso, where Archie lived next to their sister, Violet (Swanson) Paxton, husband, George, and son, Bill.

It was May when Govert and Henry started building our new house. It was down the hill from the old Stewart house in the location where their barn used to be. It was on a point out with the water in the pond on three sides of it. At last we could finally move into our new house on New Year's Day, 1951. We had new furniture in the living room. Ruebens Interiors helped me choose draperies and rugs. It was such a comfortable house! That wood-burning Lennox furnace in the basement kept every room warm. It had a fireplace in both the front room and the "family room" in the basement. We also got new beds for all three bedrooms. We had indoor plumbing–a real bathroom, and a second bathroom with a shower in the basement. The kitchen was very efficient. Visible from the kitchen window looking east was a new barn. It was just the right distance away on the level.

Across the road from the barn was the chicken house. The old barn we had used was removed and we used that spot for a garden. I raised a couple of blueberry plants, several rows of raspberries and dahlias besides our vegetables. Just to the west of this garden was a little canyon with a stream of water in it. Theodore made a dam in it up the hill so that we could have water for irrigating the garden. I had friends, the Andersons who had a nursery in town. I learned a lot about plants from them. He would dig and divide my dahlia bulbs and keep them over winter. Then he would return one of each in the spring. He encouraged me to enter some of my dahlias in the County Fair, where I did get some red and blue ribbons. Landscaping around our house was an interesting project.

Sylvia was graduated from high school that spring and was then enrolled in the local junior college. There was a feature article of our house in the Oregonian, a Portland newspaper. Charles Goodwin, who did the junior college photography in his basement, took the pictures. Sylvia was posed wearing a swimming suit in one of the pictures. It showed off the house, the pond and her. The next fall I thought that she should go to the University in Seattle. It was late November when I decided to go with her and see if she could be enrolled the next quarter. I saw to it that she had a good cello, but I do not remember what subject she wanted to pursue at the time.

I hurried with the chores that morning and somehow in doing so, I stabbed my foot with the pitchfork in the barn. It didn't bleed much, so I just ignored it; and we caught the Greyhound Bus for Seattle. On the way that foot began to hurt more and more. By the time that we arrived in Seattle, I was so sick that I thought I might faint–something that I had never done. I had a taxi take me to the nearest doctor, who gave me a tetanus shot and said that I should rest with my foot elevated. I checked into a hotel room, called Theodore, and told him my plight. He said that he would come and get us. Sylvia went to a movie while we waited. That culled her entrance to another college.

After Christmas [1952] in the new house, Sylvia did continue with classes at the junior college. I do remember that she did not feel very well. I wondered if she was getting the flu or something. She looked rather anemic. I was resting one afternoon in my bedroom when she, with her friend, David Holmes, came in to tell me the news. Sylvia was pregnant. What a shock! What to do? I thought that we should tell Mrs. Holmes. David said no to that. I must have failed as a mother.

In early March [1953], Sylvia and David had a beautiful wedding in St. Rose (Roman) Catholic Church and a reception at the Monticello Hotel. They went away to live in Seattle, where David worked at the Edmund Meany Hotel in the University District.

Maurice graduated (barely) from high school in 1954. Sometime in his high school years he took Harold Gilkey's agriculture class. His project was milking three cows. We separated the milk and sold the cream to Standard Dairy in Longview. We fed the skimmed milk to pigs. One week he wanted to go on a camping trip, and I took over the milking job. I found out that I was no dairyman. My hands would be numb before I finished. That was not a profitable enterprise. Later I always raised another calf besides the one that was born to the milk cow, plus the milk that we used. We would get the other calf from a dairyman or the auction sale. Our new barn had stalls for only six cows on its east side, and room for about 30 ewes to winter over on the west side underneath the haymow which was accessible from the road at the upper level, or by the attached ladder in the feed room/ entry between the cows and the sheep.

As yet I have not mentioned the children's music lessons. Because music was important to me, I wanted them to have the chance to learn. We were fortunate enough to have a piano. I do not remember who Sylvia's first piano teacher was. I think that it was Mordaunt Goodnough, who had a studio in the upstairs of a building downtown. I know she had a teacher in Cathlamet the year we lived on Hay Mountain. I would rather listen to her practice than to have her help me in the kitchen. Sylvia was in the orchestra at school and had trying times with the conductor, Irv Gattiker. She had her private lessons with Clement Krouse, a member of the Portland Symphony who came to town once a week to give string lessons. He once had a cello to sell and suggested that I buy it so Sylvia could practice at home. I asked Theodore if we could buy it, and he said no. I asked him if we could accept installments. Yes. So I bought it and paid for it with the money that I made on the farm.

Maurice learned to play the flute, but when he was the only boy in the flute section of the band, he wanted to change instruments to something that he thought would be more obviously masculine. Cal Storey, the band teacher, cried real tears to lose him, as he was such a good flute player. He tried saxophone and it sounded so awful that he practiced in the garage. Then he just dropped it altogether. Ted began in Ruth Aasen's Rhythm Band, a pre-school introduction to music. I think that Marie (Mrs. Charles) Goodwin was Ted's only piano teacher. I had met her years ago when she accompanied the Choral Club. Ted continued his music education on his own, without our help.

Bobby Lane was probably Maurice's first neighborhood friend, in the first house down the road. He was about the age of Sylvia. The next house, the Heitz place, was bought by the Nathan and Fredda Jo Baldwin, and their large family. They built a fine, big house and barn, and removed the old Heitz house. Tom was the oldest child and was about the same age as Maurice. At school he got acquainted with the other kids on Coal Creek. His childhood "hero" was Rab (Robert) Richards, who was older than Sylvia, and the object of her affection.

The Antilla Dairy on Carlon Loop Road was now owned by the Harvey and Adeline Handy family with five boys and no girls. All but the youngest, Jim, were older than Maurice. Jim was three months younger, and in the same graduating class. The Handy parents were getting a divorce and the boys were getting along alone there on the farm. Maurice was a senior in high school when he spent a lot of time with the Handy boys. They turned their barn into a gym for wrestling. Both Frank and Jim were champion wrestlers. When the PUD shut off their electricity Maurice borrowed one of our Aladdin lamps for them. I never saw it again. A younger boy, David Yoktorowick came to live with his sister, Fae Romph, and finish his schooling. He tagged along with these boys, but they made it rough for him. He was very shy; and rarely spoke to anyone.

After Maurice graduated from high school, he and Jim Handy joined the U.S. Army and went away to a camp in Virginia. They became paratroopers and jumped out of airplanes. Now only Ted was at home, and we had an empty bedroom. I invited a couple of missionaries to live with us and help with our little church. I heard about this organization called "Village Missions," from some people who started the Cannon Beach Conference Center. Village Missions helped small country churches like ours to survive. So, two young women came to live in our empty bedroom and have meals with us. Their names were Erma Loomer, and Delilah (Dee) Sporey. One of them said that she could milk a cow, and Ted could do the other chores, so Theodore and I decided to go on a honeymoon–some twenty years late.

Sometime in late September or early October we went to Stehekin, a remote settlement at the head of Lake Chelan, only reached by boat. One summer, Theodore's family had spent a summer up there running a saw mill. The following winter, he and his Uncle spent several months up there trapping fur-bearing animals for pelts. He told many stories of the hardships and adventures that he had that winter. The time seemed much longer than it really was. The cabin was buried deep in snow, so they had to dig their way down to the door. Food was scarce. There were hardly enough covers to keep warm at night, so that he put the towel on the bed to help a little. The wolves sometimes followed him home from his trap line. He once walked across a river on a snowy log–only to find that most of the log was snow, and he did not know how to swim. There were other narrow escapes. They sold their furs to Schumacher Fur Company in Portland. (He had an account there most of his life.)

When we arrived there on the boat, we got a room at the Lodge, a place for summer vacationers. I think that we were the only customers there at the time, as the vacation season was over. He was able to rent a vehicle–seems to me it was an old truck–so that we could drive around to the place where his Dad worked, and there were a few farms and the small school building. It had a large front porch where the schoolchildren left their snowshoes when they came to school. In the evening we went to a meeting-house, a public building of some kind where a commercial photographer was going to show some slides of winter scenes that he had taken of the area.

We were met at the door by a friendly proprietor. While Theodore was talking with him, I saw our landlady sitting over in the middle of the room waiting for the presentation. I soon went over and sat with her expecting Theodore to follow. When he finished his conversation, he didn't come. He just left; but his hat was still there, so we thought that he would soon be back. He just didn't come back. At the end I went back to the Lodge with the landlady, and found Theodore in bed and very angry with me. I could never figure out what I had done to offend him, though I reviewed the incident many times. That ended our honeymoon. We went back home to resume a more normal relationship.

The "missionary girls" were with us for several months until someone else provided them with a small cottage near the church where they had much more room. Other times I met and befriended other missionaries to the Coal Creek Church. There was John DeYoung and his sister,

New House on Stewart Creek, with Old House in background

New House & Pond on Stewart Creek

Maurice with his cows, June 1952.
Old House in background, shed in midground

Maurice after the army,
with Jim Handy (r)

Geneva, who spent her life as a missionary in Ecuador. I wrote to her regularly after she retired in Florida. Graham and Dora Adair were too helpful at times. "Oh, Graham will help you hoe the strawberries" would be a typical offer from Dora as she cheerfully volunteered her husband's services. He tried to take my place once loading logs, and wore himself out. Theodore operated the crane which picked up the logs and moved them to the truck where the truck driver loaded them and unhooked the tongs. Then he would swing the empty tongs back to me so that I could set them on another log to be loaded. The logs are heavy and move around, but Graham spent all of his time running unnecessarily.

They came to the house visiting a bit too often. One hot Sunday I particularly asked them NOT to come because we were not going to be at home. When we arrived home late that afternoon, there they were in our basement where it was always cool. Another time they stopped in when we were at dinner. Both Maurice and Jim were working with Theodore at the time and were sizing up that last piece of venison steak because they had worked hard all day. Dora swooped through the kitchen. "Oh, that's venison? I'll take that home; I'm sure that Graham has never tried it. Maurice and Jim never forgave her for that.

Maurice and Jim were fortunate to be able to stay together all the time that they were in the Army. The Army sent them to Panama, so they got to see the same places that Theodore had been. When they got out of the Army and came back home, they rented a place in Longview with Jim's brother, Frank, and went to school at the junior college. Lower Columbia Junior College (L.C.J.C.) acquired the nickname "Lucy Juicy." Since he had been in the military service, he was eligible for veteran's educational benefits. He started out majoring in engineering; but soon changed his major to forestry.

Sylvia was pregnant in Seattle. Her baby came on the twenty-first of September, a beautiful little girl, and now I was a grandmother. It must have been the following year that David decided to go to a hotel and resort management school in Washington D.C. When that happened, Sylvia and little Lorna came back home to live with us while he was gone. She got a job working at the Monticello Hotel, so Lorna was my baby for a while. She could walk and she liked to take the things out of my cupboards in the kitchen so that there was room for her to crawl in there herself. Ted just loved her. He would hold her on his lap and read to her. They would look at pictures and practice vocabulary. He was now an uncle. We enjoyed having her.

When it was time for David to come home, Sylvia didn't want to live with him any more. I told her, "No, that's not right. You must make a home for yourself now, as you promised—'In sickness and in health, for richer or for poorer'." So, they lived together in a small house on Pacific Way just down the hill from his folks' place. Ted loved to baby sit because she had a television set. Lorna soon learned the path to go visit her paternal grandparents. David worked in town for Pacific Finance for some years. Cynthia was born when they lived there, and had learned to walk before they moved to Albuquerque, New Mexico. They had often spent time with me, and I would miss them very much. David apparently got a better job offer in banking or finance, so they were gone.

It was one day in November in 1958; Maurice drove out to the house one night. Ted and I had both gone to bed. Theodore would take a little nap in the evening sitting with the newspaper on his lap, and he was still up with the lights on, maybe watching television, which we had gotten in the meantime. Maurice came and brought me into the front room where I saw a strange brunette sitting on my brown, circular, sectional davenport, who he introduced as his WIFE, Sandy. What a shock! A premonition said that this is a disaster. I had never even heard of her before. I had the impression that he was going out with Shorty (Warren) Hanson's younger sister, Roxanne, a blonde, who delivered the newspapers on Coal Creek. He would go there and play pinochle with them and hang out a lot.

The following spring, 1959, I found out why he happened to marry her. In May I acquired two more grandchildren. I went to Albuquerque to be with Sylvia and her new baby boy, Stuart. On the way, I stopped in Los Angeles to see my friend Kathryn (Davis) Hall. I stayed over maybe only one night-long enough to meet her brother. Her sister wasn't there. Her daughter, Sharon, lived with her. In her home were all of the furnishings that were so familiar to me from Doctor Davis's home in

Kelso. I kept in touch with her every year until the last time I called her on the telephone and she couldn't remember who I was any more. Her daughter, Sharon, was taking care of her. No point in confusing her; I didn't call any more.

I arrived in due time at Sylvia's. I expected to be of some help for her, but I wasn't. She was home and coping very well. They drove me around to different and interesting places. I hardly expected to be so entertained. I was just glad to spend a little time with the family–those little girls that I missed so much, and now baby, Stuart.

When I arrived back home again, there was yet another grandchild– Maurice and Sandy's baby girl, Renita. Sandy (Mason) was the daughter of Johnny Mason. The Masons were a Chinook family from Wahkiakum County. Her mother had married a number of times and currently lived in Kelso with a number of sons with different fathers. Maurice and Sandy lived in a little place behind the 20th Avenue Grocery in Longview. Thanks to Archie, he got a job at Weyerhaeuser for a while. That fall they packed up and moved to Pullman. Washington State College had become Washington State University, and he was to continue his forestry major there. They lived in a mobile home. He got a job doing some chores in the agriculture department. He even played a role in the University production of Arsenic and Old Lace. They wanted an older student to play the Doctor who ran the asylum, the final victim. Theodore never did help finance the boys' college educations. They both earned their own way through.

David got a good job offer from a bank in Bellingham, and took it. They stopped by on the way driving a small car containing a Great Dane, three children, and as much as they could possibly carry. That big dog was not welcome on the farm. It chased the livestock unless he was tied up. Stuart was a little one, and I think that I have a picture of him in a large doll buggy. Sylvia was awfully glad to be back in the damp northwest. She said that when they crossed the mountains she could smell the ocean again and just loved it.

One summer, perhaps it was just after he graduated Washington State University, Maurice brought home Sandy. She lived in the basement room. He had a job in the woods in North Bend, east of Seattle. That was close enough for him to come home occasionally. I got better acquainted with Sandy and observed her home-making style. Occasionally she would go to town for much of the day. I had to stay in the house with the kids, and could not do the outdoor work. When she took baby with her I could see that the child was worn out and unhappy. I know why. When Sandy entertained friends at my house, Baby's comfort was never a priority. It would have been so easy to just put Baby to bed when it was bed time or nap time, but she just ignored the situation. She never bothered to clean her room, and I don't remember her helping me much.

By this time there were three. Steven Jay Sterling was born 6 June 1960. The worst storm of the century, the Columbus Day Storm of 1962 found Maurice driving to Longview to meet his youngest who was born that day, Ronald Derek Sterling. Florence, Theodore's sister, named her son Ronald (Rasmussen); so the name "Ronald" had already been taken. Maurice did not like the name "Derek," so he called the baby "Mister Dee," which eventually was shortened to just "Mister." Soon he was hired to work at Hebo, Oregon out of the Ranger Station there, so they made their move to the Oregon Coast. Maurice had neglected his teeth for some time, and when he got there he was the first dental patient of a newly graduated dentist who just got his office open and did not yet have a patient or an assistant. All of his dental work got caught up again at this point.

One day when we were driving down the road, we met Ted's green 1954 Mercury coming toward us. It is only a one-lane road with turn-outs for passing. The car drove off the road. We couldn't believe it. We drove closer, and saw that Ted was not driving. He was at home. Theodore went back to the house and got the jeep and a binding chain, and Ted, and pulled it out. This is how we met Hamid Jahanmir. He told us that in Iran, the newer car has the right of way, and the older cars must yield it. He was just driving the way he would in Iran. Our car was newer, so. . . He was about 18 or 19 then, and a student at Lower Columbia–which became a "college" instead of a "junior college," and had actually attracted a handful of Iranian students. He needed American sponsors, and so Theodore filled out all the appropriate paperwork, and we sponsored him. He lived with us and worked in the woods too. He learned how to drive on the roads back in the woods so that he would not make the same mistake again. Theodore insisted that everybody knew how to back up, and Hamid was no exception to the rule.

He moved on to Seattle and school there at the University. His father and mother came out to visit us when they came to the United States to personally thank us for sponsoring him. He had little brothers that came to Longview then one at a time, and graduated from high school, Said, Jamshid, and Farshid. Hamid introduced us to Elaine, the girl that he married. The marriage did not last very long, and he never remarried. We have been included in many of their family gatherings ever since. There are cousins, and friends who never go back to Iran because of the political situation there. Hamid's father, Jalil, worked for the government there. Hamid became an American citizen, and finally graduated from the University after several years. He lives in Hawaii now; but then he ran around with Ted, Anne, Merv, Yoichi, Robert Oman, Bill Paxton, and all. Anne Hillman was a very special friend. I called her my "other" daughter. She grew up down around the Coal Creek Store and I knew her for her whole life.

I do not remember when or how it was that we learned about the magic of metal detectors. I think that it was from Sylvia and/or her new husband, David Forbes, a French horn player with the Seattle Symphony. She remembered the story she heard her dad tell when he was working for the County Road Crew. It was told by one of the older men on the crew.

It seems that there were two English men who once came to Kelso with a map describing where a relative who was then deceased had buried the gold that was brought back (to U.S.A.? I just don't know) from the north. The presumption is the Alaska gold rush. The traveling route in those days was on higher ground to avoid flooding streams and wide rivers which had no bridges. They had to ford all the water bodies. Apparently the pack animal died on route, so they had to leave the gold because it was too heavy to carry. Their map showed a very large tree which was marked with an "X." It was beside a small stream that flowed into "Oyster Creek." Theodore remembered when everybody in the country was out there looking for it. I would guess it was about 1920.

He even knew where the tree with the "X" was. The route that was used in those days was the Old Government Trail, which can still be found on Territory maps. Theodore knew where the trail was, and where it crossed the Coweeman River–which was the only water close by capable of supporting anything resembling "oysters." After all there was no sign at the time as to the name of the river that they were crossing. That metal detector was just the item that had been needed. Bert Middleton had also been involved, and that is how Theodore happened to have gleaned so much material on it. The upper Coweeman was Theodore's old home.

They bought a metal detector. Sylvia was very excited about it. We all were. Theodore and Ted went out there every day walking around looking. Finally they had the likely area re-located again. A lot of the landmarks disappear in forty years. Logging operations had come and gone. There was re-growth. Old Blackey's cabin had fallen into ruin. One week-end Maurice and Sylvia came to see how the expedition was going. It must have been March. They wanted to do this before the trees came into leaf. They had talked with old Katherine Nordvik, who showed them where the Government Trail crossed the Coweeman for sure.

Maurice went up there with them to look around. They parked the pick-up and crossed the river which had a hay field between the river and the hill where they went on the route of the old Government Trail to where Theodore remembered seeing the tree with the "X" on it after it fell down up on the hill someplace. They walked in to the next stream and all around with the metal detector without getting a peep. So they just gave up and were walking back out of the brush down the hill, and Maurice was carrying the metal detector. When they reached the flat where the hayfield was, he walked over to an old abandoned hay tedder that Jake must have abandoned years ago. He turned on the detector, and STILL could not get any response even from all that iron. So, the gold might still be there; at least we did not get any of it.

Although Maurice got quite a laugh out of it, we did use it successfully on other occasions. The Sterlings were great to bury their money. Maybe it was because of their losses in 1929 when the banks closed. Theodore buried some of Maurice's money under one of our walnut trees, and we used the metal detector to recover it, and also some of his own bills in a fruit jar. It seems incredible to me that it could find paper money in a glass jar when it was only to detect metal. Maybe something else was put with it or something. I don't know how long it was there, but I think Theodore must have put it there when he was living in the old house and the new house was moved. It didn't draw any interest. When Grandpa (Ruben) Sterling died in 1949, Grandma knew he had money buried somewhere there on the farm in Chehalis. He came into the house one day and was telling her that he had moved it from one place to another… At this point they were interrupted by a visitor. He never got around to finishing the sentence before he died suddenly one morning after breakfast. The family looked for it in every imaginable place without success. It might still be there. Where and how much, we'll never know.

We had visitors in our new house. The cousins came from Chehalis every year in May for dinner. It was kind of a family gathering. We took pictures. One occasion it was the Sterlings. I remember one time especially when my folks were here with us for a few days in September. Dad liked to fish in the pond. He also enjoyed picking blackberries. I was alone with him when he told me, "Today was the day your mother and I were married." He never forgot the true love of his life. One day I had just finished giving the front room a thorough cleaning, washed the rug, and all the furniture was out of place when a car drove up. It was my Oakesdale Pittman relatives, (Leona Pittman and her husband Herman Schwartz). I was very glad to see them, as they were easy company.

My farming activities continued year after year. Finally Theodore said, "You can't make a farmer out of me." I quit asking him to plow up the oat field. His logging was certainly the best source of income. He kept buying more land. This made the acreage of our place grow and grow. It seemed like we always had a debt to pay–until he sold a part of our land farthest from the house over on the McKee Road (off of Delameter). I think that was the year we traded a combination television/ radio/ phonograph for a baby grand piano. It was a walnut-stained mahogany Howard (made by Baldwin). It was my pride and joy even though I could not play it. Others could play it, and did play it. Theodore would always take time to plow my garden in the spring, and one year I had him plow up a bigger patch across the pond where I planted strawberries hoping to have some to sell. I added a few more rows of raspberries, and put the rest into cow beets and potatoes. I took care of the sheep and the cows most of the time. He would help me with some things like castrating and docking the lambs, or sometimes trimming their feet.

It was because of the sheep that I found a special friend, Charlie Andrews. He lived in a trailer beside his daughter's house and took care of their farm while they worked in town. They had sheep. I've listened to him tell about his life as a cowboy in California. Once when I went to see him, we went on a water-witching tour of the farm. He showed me how to do it. I bought his pet ram when they were through with it. It was a Hampshire. I was getting enough of Romney, the lambs were too small. One summer I sheared twenty-six lambs hoping they would gain more weight if they were cooler. I don't know if it helped, but I found out that the lambs' wool was not saleable. I do not remember what I did with it.

Charlie's ram was not the best for me. When lambing time came in the spring there were too many difficult births. I had to help too many. During lambing season I always went to the barn about 10:00 o'clock P.M. before I went to bed. Then I would go again about 2:00 A.M., and about 6:00 A.M., the usual chore time. No, I did not need an alarm clock. One year, one of my ewes did not dilate normally, so I called the vet. He came and delivered the lamb–dead. That poor mother suffered incredibly after the anesthetic wore off, and then she died. That happened one more time. I did not call the vet; I asked Theodore to just shoot her. I was sorry to lose her. I had raised her as a bummer lamb on a bottle and she was a kind of pet. That's the way life is on the farm.

Eventually Charlie ended up in a nursing home and I never saw him again. Years later when he died I sent the following poem to his daughter:

Heaven won't be a lonely place
If what I think is true.
A little lamb of God is there,
And some old, friendly ewe.
In those celestial pastures
Beside still waters, deep,
May the eternal future find me
With a little flock of sheep.

Dogs were the worst enemies of sheep that we had. One day a man came to our house with his dog in the back of his pick-up when the sheep were at home. That dog jumped out of the pick-up and started running after them. The man just laughed when the dog chased one of them into the pond. Theodore said, "If you don't call that dog off, I'll shoot it." The man called back his dog. Later Theodore said, "That dog will come back." Sure enough he did come back later all alone, and that was the end of that dog. Another time two dogs attacked our sheep and ripped up three of them before he put them down. The sheep were so badly wounded that if they weren't quite dead yet they would be soon, so he finished them off too. We put a notice in the store saying: FOUND–Two dogs; will owner please come and identify. A man came expecting to find his dog alive. T.H. gave him a bill for the sheep. He felt bad, of course, because he thought his dog was a wonderful dog.

I was not a good shot, like Theodore was, but I killed several myself. I enjoyed seeing the sheep come home to the barn every evening. It reminded me of the song, *Homing*:

All things come home at eventide,
Like birds that weary of their roaming,
And I would hasten to thy side–
Homing.

The Bible mentions sheep a lot, and it always irritates me when preachers call them dumb or stupid. That is not so. They are defenseless. They have short legs and can not run fast enough to escape enemies like deer. Their teeth are not designed for aggression, and they do not have a lot of strength to fight back. Once when I was working in the garden, one lone ewe came down the hill from the north pasture where the flock had been the day before. She stopped when she saw me, stood there, and just kept saying, "Baaaa! Baaaa!" I left the garden and followed her back up the hill. I took a left turn where the trail divided. She would not go that way. I circled around back to the original trail beyond where she was. As I came back to the trail, I crossed a muddy spot where I saw the footprints of a bear. I knew there would be no lamb at the spot where she was waiting for me. There was nothing that I could do to help her, so I went on home. She seemed to understand, and said no more.

Coyotes were another enemy. Theodore was a good, experienced trapper. He caught four of them in one night with his four traps. Then he skinned them out and stretched them, and sold them to Schumacher Furs in Portland, again.

Although T.H. seemed to develop an aversion to farming, we had a neighbor who just loved it. Sheldon McFadden helped with several jobs. We could get him to clean out the sheep shed–a once-a-year task that was indeed arduous. He also sheared the sheep back in the days before we had electricity for shearing. He brought a generator with him to run the shears. Maybe he also plowed, too, although Theodore would roto-till the garden.

When Lillian moved away from Sandy Bend, she went to Crescent City, California. It was a boom town then and accommodations were short. Johnny became the millwright in a redwood plywood plant there where they peeled those enormous old-growth logs big enough to drive a car through. Johnny built their house in town. There was no accommodation possible for their family cow, Lady, a rather elderly, very gentle Jersey with horns that were long and circular so that they almost re-entered her skull again. She expected to be petted when someone walked up to her. She was patient and you could even milk her outside. A stanchion was not a requirement–quite a change from Gertrude who kicked out the back of the little barn. I tried my hand at milking again like I did with Daisy during the War. Lady, with her beautiful, big eyes, became our first Jersey, and lived out the rest of her life with us. Even though T.H. was more interested in beef cows, he did not object to having her because she was already in the family. Maurice learned how to milk cows by practicing on Lady, and she became his cow for the Agricultural Project he did for Mr. Gilkey at school.

The other cow came by way of divorce. Nate Baldwin left Fredda Jo and the family. She decided to sell the place and move to Santa Barbara. Their cow, LaTissha, and Lane's cow were generally turned out of their respective barns after milking in the morning, and shooed up the road to pasture at our place for the day. In the afternoon Bobby Lane would go after the cow, and Tissha would go along home too. The next evening Nate would either "hog-call" them home by yelling real loud, or a Baldwin would go after the cow, and Lane's cow would go along home too. (It sounds funny now, but that is how things were in those days. We were all such good neighbors and friends.)

So LaTissha already knew her way around the place pretty well, all we had to do was teach her to come home to a different place. She was also a Jersey and quite a gentle, nice cow. She became the second cow for Maurice's Agricultural Project. Then a little later when Lady died, Tissha, who also had big, beautiful eyes, became our family cow. Fredda Jo and children later moved back to spend the rest of her life in Longview. T.H. was not overly happy about the Jersey situation, but, then it was a project for Maurice, and he did not say anything. I think that he was glad to be rid of the milking chore(s) and the problems with mastitis and milk fever.

Fifi, yet another Jersey cow, came into the picture when I bought her from a dairy as a "companion" calf when Tissha had a little bull calf. T.H. was unhappy with the choice. He wanted something bigger, beefier, than a cock-eyed dairy cow. I raised her from a little calf anyway, and he always resented her. Poor Tissha died that year, and rather than looking for another cow, I just kept Fifi, and got her bred. She knew the routine around there, and learned to come home when I called her; so there was no "going after the cow."

She was MY cow, and did not care much for men in general. If I were to skip a milking for some reason while out of town, I had to find a woman to milk her. Fae Romph was the woman. Fifi liked her, too;

and they got along well together. Fae and her husband, Don, became good friends. She was always there when I needed her. Fifi was the mother of several heifer calves which we raised to adulthood and sold profitably. They were pure bred Jersey, as we had Fifi bred by artificial insemination. Gloria, an aristocratic, Holstein heifer I got from a dairy on Puget Island and raised, took the top price when I sold her at the auction in Chehalis. I always turned the cows out of the barn in the evening during the summer and nice weather. One morning I went out to do the chores and milking and found Fifi upside down in the canyon–dead as she could be. She must have been running and then stepped in a mole hole that threw her over on her back so that she could not get up again. That is all it takes to kill a cow.

What did we do for milk then? I don't remember. Usually I bought bull calves to raise for beef. Once we went to a dairyman in the Elochoman Valley expecting to buy a bull calf. When we got there he asked if we would mind taking this heifer that was half Black Angus from a Holstein heifer. I did. We called her Mavis after the character in Dark at the Top of the Stairs. Unlike the other cows, she was a dark, glossy black, which stood out like a bear. Despite her size–she was a big girl!–she was very tame and gentle, and became a real pet. I would go to the barn and call her at milking time, and she would come home from clear across the canyon. She was the last cow I ever milked. All these farming activities over the years made me appreciate James Herriot's books about *All Creatures Great and Small*.

Theodore, Ted, RosaMae, baby Lorna, on front steps of new house

Sylvia (Sterling) Holmes, David Holmes, baby Lorna

Hamid Jahanmir with RosaMae wearing jacket from Iran.
Ted's car in background, the 1954 Mercury

(l-r) Sylvia, Bill Paxton, Maurice, and Ted playing piano, January 1972

Part Four – Later Married Life
(1970's – 1980's)

When Maurice graduated from college, he got a job with the forest service at Hebo, Oregon. They provided a small, but comfortable home there, and they found good friends. They were not too far away from us, so they could come home once in a while and we would also go there. Hebo is a tiny hamlet named after Mount Hebo, which has a lot of weather data gathering equipment up there. There are some surprising high winds up there. This is the Siuslaw National Forest on the northern Oregon coast.

One summer when Mister was a baby, they came and I saw that he had diarrhea, and his little bottom was raw from not being cleaned and changed often enough. They left him with me for a while and I got him cured up. Then I told them that the doctor said that they shouldn't feed him watermelons and just everything; stick to baby food–I was the doctor. It must have been the following Christmas that Sandy came to Kelso early. They usually spent the holidays with us. Maurice would come later. Instead, he got a letter from her saying that she would never come back to Hebo again, and she wanted a divorce. Maurice was in shock for days. He couldn't work with visions of the loss of his children and the probability that they were not getting very good care in his mother-in-law's filthy house.

I can't remember all of the activities and adventures and legalities that he went through with the help of friends at this point. Our old neighbors, the Lane family, came in very handy. Betty Lane Oman lived for a time with her folks, so her son, Robert, was right there too. We have always been close friends. Sandy did not know Robert. Maurice got him to follow her around and blend into the crowd, and he was good at it. He kept track of her and reported in to Maurice all her activities. Needless to say, we rejoiced when he did get custody of his children. They went back to Hebo with him, and an older woman, I think she was a widow, was their housekeeper for a while.

Sylvia came from Bellingham occasionally. Once when she came with the children, she left all the suitcases at home a couple hundred miles away, so she did not stay long on that trip. I went up there once to help her do some work in a bedroom, redecorating. Stuart was a little tyke riding up and down the driveway on a tricycle where he took a bad spill. He didn't seem to recover; instead, he got sick and sicker. It was time for me to go home on the train when David (Holmes) took him to the hospital. When I got home they called and told me that Stuart had spinal meningitis. Ted heard that it was always fatal, so we were worried about it, but Stuart pulled through and was very normal.

Where was Ted? He stayed with Lu and Jack and graduated from high school in Oakesdale, and worked on farms there during the summer. Then he went to college here, where both he and Maurice graduated on the same night. Then he lived in Seattle to do musical comedies for the World's Fair. The Theatrical Company went broke; and he came home that same spring when my dad died, 1962. It must have been sudden. He was found under the apple tree. Ted went back to school in Bellingham for a while. He sang with a male quartet at Western and somehow the accompanist, Dave Forbes, met Sylvia. I think they were both in the Bellingham Symphony at the same time. Eventually she divorced Dave Holmes, and married Dave Forbes, who was ahead of Ted in school. When Dave graduated they moved to Bainbridge Island, as Dave played French horn for the Seattle Opera and Symphony.

Lorna was written up in the newspaper when she lived in Albuquerque as being the youngest Public Library cardholder. Now, as a high school student there on Bainbridge Island, she went to Germany as an exchange student for a year. Sylvia had various projects there to help increase their limited income–especially after the metal detector did not locate the gold. A beautiful child, Angela Rose, was born to them on April 13th 1968. We went there when she turned two so that she and Grandpa Sterling (T. H.) could celebrate their birthdays together. His birthday is April 14th. Cynthia went and lived with her dad, Dave Holmes, and his new wife and adopted son in southern California about the time Lorna came back from Germany.

It was sometime in the sixties that we joined the Farm Forestry Association. Theodore did some logging for Alban (?) Nelson down on Fall Creek, and he must have been a member, too. Maybe they were competing with each other. The Columbus Day Storm of 1962 took down enough timber in various patches to make it foolish not to go up the hill and salvage as much of it as he could. That meant building the necessary roads to accommodate the log truck to haul out the loads.

The road past the haymow was continued way back up the hill and became a network of roads for hauling, yarding, and/or traversing to the next patch of down timber. They worked here on the home place for a long time just cleaning up the mess and re-planting with little trees. Then he decided that he could thin timber as well as the next person, and proved it. In the mid-1960's we went to the annual meeting in the spring, and he was given the Tree Farmer of the Year Award, which was written up with a picture in The Longview Daily News.

Bonneville Power and Light bought a right of way easement through the place in the late 1940's for the construction of a power line. Nothing was done for years. Then in about 1963, they decided to build the line, so a stripe of vegetation about 125 feet wide was removed for miles to accommodate the lines which were hung from tall metal towers which held three lines twenty five feet apart from horizon to horizon. They were obliged to pay for the trees that were of marketable size, that were condemned. This gave Theodore another project. Bonneville used his roads on our property. They were already in. This proved to be only the nose of the camel, however, as shortly thereafter we were informed that the Department of Energy had decided to augment the existing line with another line parallel to it. This is a case of Public Domain. We could not fight the United States of America. The line went in. The barn was under the easement, so it had to be moved east to a suitable location because there was no place on the west side of the lines to locate it. All the flurry of activity that we went through for the first line was repeated on the second line. It was quite a jaunt to the barn after it was re-located at approximately the same level as the house.

That was not the end of the story. We got another letter that there would be another augmentation, and this one hit the house. Lucille advised us to take a cash settlement and just move out and let them have it. There did not seem to be an end. We agonized over the situation a good deal. The house was moved. The garage was severed and placed down where the old sheep shed and garden were. The house was placed on big steel girders which were leveled, and there it sat. I moved to town. Theodore and the dog, Clyde, moved back into the old house so that the place would not be abandoned. At last the old Stewart house was pulled out of its location and he dug a hole for a new basement to be poured so that the new house would just barely fit outside the west boundary of the danger zone. Sherm sized it all up and measured everything and said that it would fit there, and it did.

Clarence Johnson was Theodore's mechanic, friend, and hunting partner. He had a little shop along Ocean Beach Highway beside his modest home. He nearly always wore a welding cap, and was called "Johnson," not Clarence. Even his wife called him Johnson. He could fix anything. He even tuned his own piano. He was a loyal and faithful friend. Sooner or later he was likely to be called to come to the logging site and fix something. He had a mobile unit in the back of the Jeep pick-up that we ended up buying from him, because it would go anywhere. I think that he was the one who called Theodore "T. H.," rather than "Chirp" or Theodore. That was how Theodore signed his name on a check, so it pretty well stuck. Johnson had two sons, Floyd and Ted, who both worked in heavy machinery, and were a little older than Sylvia. Floyd drove gravel truck and could spread a load beautifully; Ted Johnson started a logging outfit, and hired Theodore as a cat operator with his chokerman, Ted, to work for him in an old-growth setting in the summer of 1961.

Now we were prospering. We had no more debts. We sold a large tract of timber to Ted Johnson. I was upset because it was worth more than Theodore asked for it. Ted made a fortune, wasted all of his money, his wife left him, and he became a poverty-stricken drunkard. We still had the land, and sold it at a good price to Evenson Logging Co., a family company, who re-planted it to Douglas fir. Theodore decided that it was time to make a will, and gave certain tracts of land to our children. Each forty-acre tract was described on a separate piece of paper. Then little Mister was given the job of mixing up the papers and then handing one paper to Sylvia, one to Maurice, and one to Ted. Then the results were recorded at the Courthouse.

The Forest Service transferred Maurice out of Hebo. He left his fishing partner, John Baker, and the community that he grew to love there with great reluctance. He so enjoyed living there; the people and the place. Now he was moved to the Wenatchee National Forest, and he lived in Leavenworth. Nina was about ten years old when she came to live with me for a year. She went to school in Longview. I saw that she had piano lessons, took her to a dancing class, and treated her like my own daughter. At the end of the year she went back to Leavenworth. Maurice had a special friend in Leavenworth, a school teacher, who tried to help him with his children–especially Nina, who seemed to be entering a rebellious age.

I always listened to Bible studies on the radio while I was working in the kitchen: J. Vernon McGee, on *Through the Bible*, Warren Wiersbe, then another I found from Portland must have been on Sundays, or evenings, when Theodore was at home, because he listened too. Dwight Custus, pastor of Central Bible Church in Portland, was the speaker. We started going to church there regularly for quite some time, so you get acquainted with a few people. Theodore decided that he wanted to give quite a large sum of money to the church, and was advised to give it to Multnomah School of the Bible, which was an extension of the church. That was how we became involved with Multnomah. Floyd Bolich, Pete Scruggs, and Willard Aldrich became special friends. We had a trust written up with Multnomah's lawyer, Nelson Repsold. Theodore went to see Floyd several times after he retired and was in poor health before he died.

We visited in Willard Aldrich's home in Vancouver where he lived for many lean years while his large family was growing up. The city grew up around his place, and it became a commercial area rather than a residential one. We went to his new home out in the country. He had a fish pond like ours. Woodworking was his hobby, and, like Theodore, he liked the woods and fields. We often had lunch with Pete and Irene when they had errands in the north. They would call us and we would meet them in a designated restaurant by the freeway in Kelso, or they would come out to our place.

I do not remember just when it was that I began to have "problems." I just remember related incidents. Once we took baby Mister back to Sandy and Maurice in Pullman because I felt very tired and overworked.

One day Dick Umbaugh came into the kitchen with Theodore. I was standing at the sink when he came and put his arm across my shoulders. I don't remember what he said; but I thought–"If only Theodore would do that just once, and tell me that he appreciated my efforts with a little affection, it would mean the world to me!" He never did. Problems began to develop. One day while everyone was off to work as usual, my day was ahead of me as usual. What shall I do? The washing? Mow the lawn? Hoe weeds? Clean house? I felt overwhelmed; and sat down on the davenport and cried most of the day. I gathered my wits about me in time to do what had to be done–fix dinner and do the chores–so nobody would know what my day was like. This happened occasionally.

Then I couldn't eat very well. Theodore took me to a clinic in Portland where they must have examined my whole digestive system, plus anything else. The doctor looked at me strangely and said, "There is nothing at all the matter with you." The word "depression" was never heard of. He suggested that I change my routine, go out more, and do something different for a change. Yes, I went out to dinner and couldn't swallow anything. Usually that happened at home, but I finally got over that. Life went on. After my father died in April of 1962, I went with my mom and her brother, Ed, to Minnesota. That was different and helpful. We had a good time there. First stop in Minneapolis to see cousin, Nora, and her husband; then on to Kilkenny, where most of the relatives are.

The cousins who drove us around were retired old farmers. Ed and his cousin remembered the songs they used to sing together when they were young. It was a fun trip. Then we took the bus down to Missouri to see Bill Pittman. He was alone. I don't know when his wife, Elsie died. It was interesting to see how he lived and be there for a while. Then back home.

In the seventies, I think Lorraine and Winston were living in Portland. I remember riding with them from Portland to a family gathering in Latah. Usually Theodore went with me on these trips. We must have seen them sometimes, because we went with them and the group from her brother, Sherman's church in California, on a tour of Europe and the Holy Lands. I was surprised that Theodore would–or could–afford to spend the money. We were prospering. He enjoyed that trip the most because of Lorraine's enthusiasm and excitement. We rode with them from Portland to San Francisco, where we met our group, flew to New York, on to Paris, then to Berlin, where we stopped for a time to view the destruction caused by the war. The Berlin Wall was there in place. We went through "check point Charlie" to board another plane for Moscow, USSR. We were there for several days. I remember the subway. I was so afraid of becoming separated from our group in that place.

We visited many interesting places there, and then flew on to Egypt where we rode camels to the pyramids, walked down into one, and visited a museum where there were relics from Tutankhamen's Tomb. Theodore didn't want to leave there, but there were other sights to see before we flew on to Tel Aviv, then by bus to Jerusalem. While there, we visited the desert around the Dead Sea, Mossada, the Sea of Galilee, and surrounding area. Then we went on to Greece to explore the ruins there. We boarded a ship that took us to visit the Islands. Unfortunately we encountered a storm that evening, and most of the people got sick; but not me. I grew up on a swing. Theodore was fine for a while and laughed about everyone throwing up. A little later he was sick and vomited his teeth into the toilet. Of course they were retrieved and thoroughly cleaned. We must have gone on from there to Italy. In Rome we went to see Aida presented outdoors at the Coliseum. One evening we went to Sorrento, and spent some time exploring Pompeii. Now it is time to come home.

When winter came, Maurice came for Christmas and brought us some apples from Leavenworth. He was now working for the Wenatchee National Forest. He lived there for years and grew to be unhappy with his job–which had become mainly policing park visitors rather than cruising timber or supervising thinning or logging operations, building roads, etc. He managed his finances very well. He had money invested at Merrill Lynch. He owned a house in Hebo. Jim Handy, his best friend, had bought a hamburger joint at Newport and started a chain. Now he saw an opportunity to buy a large restaurant in Albany, and he talked with Maurice about the possibility of forming a partnership. Maurice was given an interesting assignment by the Forest Service in the meantime. He was asked to prepare a study to discuss a problem that he would research: Why the best and most capable forest rangers leave the U. S. Forest Service. Maurice went through the records and talked with former employees. He really heard a lot of stories, put them all together, wrote up his analysis, and included his resignation paper as the last page.

He took a mixology class in bartending that was given in Portland so that he would be knowledgeable there, as Jim had never run a bar before, and this place had a bar. They went ahead and got the big restaurant in Albany. He used the investment money to pay for it. I do not know if they were "equal" partners as to their percentages and all. They were doing some remodeling on the building. It was early spring, and Maurice asked if the children could stay with me and finish the school year. He and Jim could get the remodel done and the restaurant going. He would then have time to find a house to move into. It may have been in March during spring vacation when they moved in with me. Maurice probably had his furniture in storage, as he and Jim were living in a motel room, and most of their time was spent at the business.

For some reason, he was with us for a few days in April–maybe just to see the children. He left and went back to Albany on Friday. On Saturday morning the telephone rang while the kids were having breakfast. It was the Albany Police Department saying that Maurice had been shot. He was in the hospital in critical condition. What a shock! There was not much to say. We looked at each other and got the kids fed. The telephone rang again, and Theodore answered it. The gunshot wound to his head was fatal. What a birthday present for Theodore! His favorite son! He went to Albany with the pick-up to bring him home. Maybe Ted went with him. Recalling this day, I still feel the anguish of the moment.

Life went on. There were chores to do; meals to cook. I sent the children off to school on Monday as usual, and perhaps that was the wrong thing to do. Theodore planned to bury him at the Claquato Cemetery in Chehalis where we had lots. I just couldn't bear to have him so far away. He had never lived in Lewis County! I would have liked to have him buried right in our yard. Ted bought lots at Bunker Hill Cemetery, a place much like the Latah Cemetery, but much closer.

Theodore reluctantly consented. I wish now that Theodore had had his way. We arranged for his very non-commercial Funeral to take place in Kelso on Wednesday. His friends came from Hebo to officiate with a very brief and simple message. His coffin was made of weathered hand-split cedar boards that came off of Ratcliff's barn (a Handy neighbor.) After the carpenter built it, Virginia Mounce upholstered the inside of it so it was very nice. Anne Hillman made the floral spray out of dogwood, sword ferns, maybe apple blossoms—just local plants that were growing out in the woods, and pretty at that time—not something from a florist. A flute player played that same Mozart Sonata second movement that we all heard him practice and play so many, many times. It was all very simple and beautiful; but he was gone. From then on he was forever—missing.

The next day we resumed our schedules. The chores needed doing, the children went off to school; but Theodore did not go off to work. We found out that Maurice had stayed there at the restaurant overnight to apprehend thieves who had acquired a habit of stealing steaks. Come to find out, IT WAS THE POLICE who climbed up the exterior stairs and entered the back way. The police had killed him. The steaks went for their entertaining. Maurice fired his gun into the ceiling. Was it to warn and frighten them, or did his shot come after he was hit and falling to the floor? Were words exchanged? That time of the morning it is pretty easy to see someone crawling in a window. When did he wake up? The police allege that he was killed during a possible crime investigation. So who called the Police? They parked right beside his car. If they were investigating a crime, why did they not check on the ownership of the vehicle through the license-plate check like they always do when investigating? There are too many questions here. The Police were the thieves, as well as the killers.

The first day of school after the funeral, I got a call from somebody saying that the children would not be coming home on the bus; their mother had come and taken them to Astoria. I truly cried aloud in anguish. Their clothes were all at my house. Would they be properly cared for? Maurice had especially mentioned in his will that the children be with me because their mother would not provide a good home for them.

No more work around our place. The loading rig just sat there at the landing, idle. We engaged a lawyer firm in Portland to sue the City of Albany for the wrongful death of our son. It took a lot of time running back and forth. We were disappointed with Jim as a witness at the time of the trial. I guess we didn't have much of a chance against the city. The lawyers took a chance on accepting a portion of what they hoped to win for us as a partial payment, so it did not cost us a fortune.

That was not the end of trouble. Bonneville had condemned the third strip of land through our property and demanded that we move our house. The second line had required that we move the barn to the east away from the house, but we could still see the barn, and just put up with the extreme distance. Now where could we put the house? We sued Bonneville for considerably more money than they offered, and won the case. Theodore measured the spot where the old Stewart house was still located a few feet off of the proposed new right of way. There was room, and we could move our house up there. Of course the west entrance of the living room, viz. the front door, would not be accessible from the driveway, because now the approach would be from the east rather than the west. The garage would need to be altered as well to accommodate the vehicles coming from the opposite direction. We could see that the back door through the garage was going to get the lion's share of traffic entering the house through the utility room; but we could still use that excellent water supply that we always had.

Theodore engaged a house-moving company in Vancouver to do the job. Of course they were busy and couldn't do it right away; and we were happy to delay as long as possible. The deadline finally came when authorities came from Olympia to inform us that the house must be moved off of the right-of-way by a certain date or else they would begin to demolish it. Those city people seemed to think that we were way far back in the woods. One man asked if we ever saw any bears. Theodore looked over at the game trail across the power line right-of-way on the hill south of the house. "Yes," he casually replied. "There's one right there," pointing it out to him. It was remarkable how that ever happened, as we had not seen a bear in years.

We had to get busy and move everything out of the basement. The moving crew moved our house off of the foundation, divided the garage off of the house, and took it down at the corner, then parked the house in the yard along the road. We rented an apartment downtown on Seventh Avenue through the winter. There were still daily chores to do on the farm. Theodore had the old kitchen stove re-installed in the old Stewart house again, so he could stay there part of the time. There was still water in the sink up there, too. I was within walking distance of downtown, and I took some sewing classes. I had made flannel shirts for Theodore and the boys through the years, and thought that I might learn something new.

Through the years Archie would come out and bring us a fish now and then. He had his own boat and went often. Sometimes Theodore went with him, but he and his boat were standard fixtures in the Cowlitz/Columbia area. He retired from Weyerhaeuser and spent even more of his time fishing and gardening. One day he went out in the morning to fish at the mouth of the Cowlitz. He spent the morning in the Columbia. A friend on another boat came over to see if he got anything. Arch had not had any luck, so he told the friend that he was going to pull into the Cowlitz and try there, which he did. Later, the friend saw the boat on the Cowlitz and called to him to see if he caught anything. Unable to rouse a response, he pulled his boat over to find Archie in his boat—dead.

When all of our efforts failed to get Maurice's children back, Sandy must have felt safe enough to move back to Kelso for a while. During that time Nina chose to come over and live with me at the apartment. Ted was working at Troy Laundry and living in a small rented house on Eighth Avenue, not far away. Stuart spent some weeks with us in December so that he could play the part of Amahl in the local production of *Amahl and the Night Visitors*, a Christmas opera, over at the college. Nina was just home from having her tonsils removed and in bed one day. I brought her a bowl of soup for her supper in the evening, and Stuart threw a pillow at her, spilling soup all over her bed. I was really mad, and sent him into the bedroom while I cleaned up the mess. When I went in there to get him for supper, the room was empty. He had crawled out the window and gone over to Ted's house.

When spring came, we found a place out on Ocean Beach Highway, and moved there to be closer to home. While I was living there I had company. My sister, Lucille, was no longer a widow. She stopped in with her new husband, Fritz Allert. Another day I got a call from a man in Astoria saying that he was tired of babysitting, and could he bring the children to me—their mother, Sandy, had been drunk for a week. Of course they came, and I thought the situation would help us to get permanent custody of the children. It didn't, but Nina stayed with me. In the meantime Theodore was fixing up the house so that he could live in it all blocked up like it was for a while.

At the apartment, Nina was spending a lot of time visiting kids next door. It seemed all right to me. I didn't expect her to help me much with the house work. One evening she said she was going to babysit for someone farther away. Theodore said, "Hmmm; I think I'll go and check up on her." Sure enough, he was right. No baby sitting—a party of some sort; and he brought her home again. Once she went next door—or so I thought—in the evening and she never did come home until the next day. She would not say where she had been except that she was next door. Fortunately we could soon move back into our own house back on the farm again. She simply would not live there, and went back to Astoria. Her mother couldn't do anything with her, either. She was put into a foster home.

Theodore and I went on another trip with Sherman Williams' church group that summer, and we took Cynthia with us. Sherman's two daughters went along too, and they were near her age. This time, we went to the Scandinavian countries: first Bergen, in Norway, where we visited the home of the composer Edvard Grieg, who wrote the music for *Song of Norway*. Then we went by bus through the mountains to historic places along the way to Sweden, Denmark, the Alps in Switzerland, up the Rhine River, then across to Venice and St. Mark's Square, and back to northern Italy on our way home. Sherm and Minnie Sterling stayed in our house and took care of the place while we were gone.

Then we had another winter with the house not very comfortable. Theodore insulated the furnace heat pipes as best he could so that we could use the furnace to heat the house a little better instead of just the fireplace. He must have connected us to the sewer system, too, so we could use the plumbing. It must have been in the spring when we got the old Stewart house moved off to the side, and the old woodshed, porch, and cooler-room destroyed and cleared away so that he could dig the basement so that we could pour all the appropriate cement and all. Finally they day came when all that heavy equipment was secured to those steel beams under the house. Inch by inch they began pulling it up that steep hill and into place over that hole that would be our basement. There were workmen there a long time putting up the concrete walls for the basement, building up the chimney where our family room fireplace had been.

Nothing was really as nice as it had been. There was no basement bathroom any more. The furnace was not as close to the chimney, so all the ducts had to be changed to fit the furnace. Finally it was finished and we could live comfortable through the winter. He wanted to move the old house down in the former driveway, but without skids under it, it began to pull apart. Someone came and took it apart for all of the beautiful old-growth lumber that it contained.

With our house up the hill in the seventies, Theodore had seven hives of bees. Extracting honey is no small job, and always done on a hot day in the basement. We had honey to sell. One year there was a swarm that was particularly hostile. Theodore mowed the lawn in his bee-protection clothes. I sneaked out the back way to pick raspberries down in the lower garden. I came back the same way, but they found me before I could get into the house again. We couldn't put up with that indefinitely. After about a week of that, we had to kill them. I like bees; my grandpa Pittman did too. He had a commercial apiary—some thirty swarms—at his farm in Minnesota. I went there for a visit with Ted when he was small and had not entered school yet; and Grandpa was old—about ninety. He would sit in his chair in the yard and watch the bees. He recognized when they were about to swarm. He always seemed to know just what they were doing.

The Stewarts left their orchard behind them. They had used standard rootstocks which led to large trees, as was the custom at the time. The apple trees were planted in a north/south line at about twenty-five to thirty foot intervals. They also had a Royal Anne cherry tree that was a bit out of line. It was getting old and senile. It died in our first decade. The five apple trees were: standard Gravenstein, Twenty-ounce Pippin, Wolf River, and two trees of Waxen. I thought that the Gravenstein was a Duchess of Oldenburg like Papa had on the farm, but I soon learned that Gravenstein was a standby apple west of the Cascades at that time. It was the first to begin to ripen and ripened over some weeks so that they were not all ripe at the same time. The kids just loved them. They were good for cooking, eating out of hand, and all, but they did not store well. Twenty-ounce Pippin, as the name might imply, was a large, greenish cooking apple often weighing more than a pound, and kept better than Gravensteins.

Wolf River apples were popularized by the Northern Pacific Railroad because they were about the same size as the Twenty-ounce, and retained their good looks even when baked and served in individual glass dishes on the dining cars. They were a beautiful rather light red with very white flesh; crisp, but rather bland when eaten out of hand. Two trees of Waxen apples, the best keeper, were a little much. Theodore used the bottom tree as a grafter, and put other varieties on it. Waxens were developed at Washington State University for western Washington sites around the first decade of the century. They were yellow, inclined to over-produce, and had a most unique stem which was not like any other apple of my acquaintance. The suffered a great deal by comparison with the Gravensteins, which were gone by the time Waxens came ripe in mid to late October.

Theodore wondered what scions to graft onto the grafter Waxen tree. Old Mrs. Merkel took him way back in the woods between Coal Creek and Mosquito Creek to an abandoned orchard that she knew about there. They had to walk both ways from her place. She lived between Ratcliffe's and Handy's. I do not know what made these apples so desirable. The limbs were cut off, and he grafted on: Yellow Transparent, Honey, and Red Astrakhan. There was another limb and no scion for it, so he grafted on another Northern Spy. Twenty-five years later he discarded the Honey and Red Astrakhan grafts and installed Red Gravenstein instead.

We planted some trees of our own over on the west side of the old Stewart house. Theodore was sure that the kids would like McIntosh, a favorite from his youth in Pennsylvania. Northern Spy was his favorite "keeping apple" for the winter, so we planted it. I thought Jonathan would be good, so that went in. He also wanted a Green Gage plum, like the one that used to be at Catlin School. They had torn it down and built another school in a different location. Standard Dairy built a plant on the site and removed the tree. Now we had one. I also planted an apricot out of ignorance. The frost killed it.

Whitney Crab was a good pollinator and the apples were good for pickling. There was another tree or two, perhaps. The McIntosh, and all members of the Fameuse apple family, were at a biological disadvantage in the climate, and fell a victim of anthracnose, a disease. Theodore quick cut off most all of the McIntosh and grafted on Winter Banana, and that tree became a grafter, too. One time my dad came over for a visit in the early spring when Ted was about twelve or so. The two of them pruned the orchard. From then on, even the old trees did not get senile or overgrown, because Ted had really learned how to prune apples well, and kept the trees in good shape.

When we moved into the new house down by the pond, we planted more apples in the gardens that we vacated. We had three Italian prune trees along the road, and pie cherries on the railroad bench down by the pond. We had a couple of pear trees, and planted another Gravenstein in the back yard behind the garage. We vacated the garden which was all fenced, so I planted some sweet cherry trees, and an odd assortment of apples. Blue Pearmain and Keswick Codlin were heritage apple varieties that the Woodwards brought with them from Canada when my father was a boy. I planted a Jefferis tree because it was so good when I was a child, and quite a disappointment at this location. Ida Red I could hardly keep alive because of disease. Almata had problems with animals. Spartan was a good apple, but not a very healthy tree. Melrose was an unknown, but proved itself quite a success for the experiment. I planted a King of Tompkins County in my old flower bed, and it became the "standard" October apple like the Northern Spies were the November apple, and Gravenstein was the September apple.

Sometime in the seventies Mervyn and Ted gathered up about a pick-up load of apples and took them down to an old man who let them borrow his cider press, and showed them how to make cider for a percentage of the juice. They collected jugs and all and each had a lot of cider. Ted did not have any place to put it, so I canned some, and some we froze, the rest we left out and drank. Then we got our own cider press—brand new. This was a continuing project every year, as we had so many apples. The Waxens were good for tart cider. We made different blends. Gravenstein was sweet. Since we had about four or five Gravenstein trees, they were the backbone of most of it. How we enjoyed that!

Usually Theodore was very careful and lucky as regarding industrial accidents in the woods. He did have a bad hit on the head when we were living in the old Stewart house. Archie brought him home, and he had to just stay in bed for a while until he was better. He got the stitches out and healed up real well. You couldn't even see the scars. He habitually wore a tin hat from then on, and insisted that the boys and everyone out there in the woods did. This did leave him with problems with his neck. He went as far as McMinnville to go to a chiropractor to get relief. I thought that it would help if he just would not go to sleep in the rocking chair and have his head bounce around in his sleep so. He also had many times of back trouble. In the 1960's he spent some time in the hospital. I don't know what they could do for him. Archie brought him home that time. He had another spell the year I was in the apartments. He just stayed in bed for a few days, and I had to go out there to take care of him and do the chores until he could come to town again. Was it caused by moving all that stuff out of the basement?

I think it was in the spring of 1973—the house was functional up the hill from the former location—when we made our third (and last) trip to Europe. I think that Mister had just graduated from high school—he was the only one of Maurice's kids to actually graduate from high school. He came for a visit about that time. We had him and a girl from the Salvation Army stay on the place while we were gone. It was June, and Mister was supposed to keep the garden watered. This time we went to Spain—Madrid and Toledo. Remember the expression "Holy Toledo"? It's because there are so many cathedrals there. We visited all of them.

During a stop overnight in Italy, we found out that something was amiss with my passport or visas, and Iraq denied me access, so I could not enter and go to Baghdad like everyone else in our tour group was going to do. Next we stayed in Beirut. Sherman offered to stay there with me while the others went on to Iraq; but Theodore stayed with me instead. Another tour group came into the hotel at that time. We were having dinner in the late afternoon on the seventh floor. Suddenly a shot was fired through the window into the ceiling. During the next day we wanted to walk across the street and out on the beach of the shores of the Mediterranean, but we were advised not to do it as it was too dangerous. Our group came back from Iraq in the late afternoon. They had seen Ur—where Abraham came from.

The next morning we flew on to Amman, Jordan. We were on the seventh floor of that hotel too—near the palace. Theodore sat on the toilet seat to lean over and tie his shoe. The toilet lid cracked, damaging his back. All he could do was lie down on the bed for a while to recover. The window was open and the door was open for the air. I went down to ask for his dinner to be brought to our room. When I came back I saw that the wind had blown the door shut. My keys were inside the room. Sherman said that they would have another set of keys at the desk. While we were waiting, a man came with Theodore's dinner. Word came that there was not another key at the desk. What to do?

Sammy, our guide, finally went into the room next door and out on their balcony. From there he jumped across the open space seven floors above the ground, over to our balcony, then through the open window into our room, where he let us in again through the door. That's how Theodore finally got his dinner in Amman. The next day we were scheduled to go by bus across the desert to Petra, the ancient city in the rocks. Theodore went with Sherman to some place and waited for us to come back. Theodore's back must have recovered. I think we went on to Venice, Milan, and home.

As I read back in my old diaries, I realize what a busy person I was. Before we moved the house up the hill, I had an incubator in the basement where I hatched goose eggs and duck eggs. My neighbor had ducks. We sold the babies. I didn't hatch chicken eggs. We had to sell the incubator when we had to move everything out of the basement and move the house. I raised a bunch of chickens there for fryers, dressed them all (Theodore cut off their heads), and put them in the chest freezer along with other meat and vegetables. The upright freezer was not big enough. I took care of the livestock most of the time. It was a profitable enterprise. Theodore went with me to the auction sales to buy calves; he also hauled animals to market with the pick-up. If our load was too big, we hired someone else to do it.

What were the years that I helped load logs? Theodore was harvesting some alder on the Phare place (just south of us) and Joe Zdilar was working with him. I helped load one load when Joe wasn't there. It was quite a process. I hooked the tongs onto a log, then I climbed onto the truck to un-hook the tongs, then climbed down from the truck and over on the cold-deck to select another log, and hook the tongs again. Ted did it the easy way by riding the log, and hanging onto the empty tongs and being swung back to the log pile again. I got more and more tired because the more logs we loaded onto the truck, the harder it was to climb up and down again. Ben Fisher worked in the woods with or after Verle Flatt. After Ben, must have been Ted.

When winter came and outdoor activities were limited, I had sewing to do. I made several quilted quilts; appliqued tulip design by hand. I had room to set up the quilt frame in the spare room. I sewed shirts, nightgowns, or more quilt patches for the church quilting projects. I knitted sweaters for each of the boys. I wonder what Steve and Mister did with theirs? I often had company. Cynthia and her neighbor girl, Sandy Jernigan, spent their spring vacation with us, and maybe more time in the summer. That is when I became "Grandma" to Sandy Jernigan too. Another friend that joined the girls was Beth Rowland, MaryLynn Richards' daughter. She was a special friend for quite a few years. Then, of course, there were Maurice's children on their vacations and holidays.

Anne Hillman came out so often after work or about suppertime. She worked for the Bon Marche in Longview. Then she was transferred to the main store in Seattle. After a while she transferred again back to Longview. She was an artist who started there doing advertisements in the newspaper. Gradually her responsibility and salary grew. She came by so often that she just felt like a daughter. Then she dropped in from Seattle with her Iranian friend, Reza, the cousin of Hamid, who was later her "husband." He also became our friend. I have several gifts which he brought to me from Iran. (They made their trip the year after Ted went over there.) After she made the trip to Iran to visit the family there, they became estranged. Back in Longview again, she drove me to the hospital so often to visit Theodore when he had heart surgery in Portland. She married an Indian, Jaswant Ratoul, a nautical engineer. They had a terrible time getting him legally into the country. He went all over the world working on ships. It seems that they had so little time together before her untimely death, but that is her story.

Angie was with me off and on quite a bit. One week I needed her especially when I fell, sprained my ankle, maybe twisted my knee, as sometimes happened. I couldn't walk for about a week. I think we had to can beans that week. She was a good helper. Maurice's children were not. Her father, Dave Forbes, came once to get her, and explained that he would like to get custody and keep her with him so that she would have a more stable home life. Sylvia was not behaving responsibly. He was right, but didn't pursue the idea with any legal action that I was aware of. He was married (again) at that time and later divorced again.

Sylvia had moved to Bainbridge Island from Bellingham in the mid-1960's. I do not remember when she moved from Bainbridge Island to

Ballard, or from Ballard to Issaquah, to Belfair, to Packwood, to Randle, etc. I wonder if SHE can remember all the places she lived, and when she lived there. I doubt it. When Cynthia graduated from High School, she went to live with her father in California where she finished college and got a job teaching school. We went on a trip to San Diego on the train. Dave and his wife entertained us royally—took us to all the local places of interest. I went to church with them, where I met Mrs. Tim Lahay. She was just beginning her "Concerned Women for America" project. We went to Fallbrook, where Cynthia was teaching home-ec, and I visited her sewing class. In the summer, her adopted brother, Scott, came with Cynthia to see us. He was interested in our farm. I wrote to Robin and talked to her on the phone. We were all friends until Cynthia married a person they disapproved of. Lorna was also pursuing her education in far away places, but made frequent appearances.

It was in the seventies, while the house was up the hill, that the men from the Gun Club came and asked Theodore to sell to them the property that they had been renting for several years. I said, "NO, NO!" But he ignored me. These people were his friends; and Theodore always had his own way about buying and selling land.

So he measured out a strip of land over in the oatfield, where they had been shooting. I remember the day we sat in our kitchen to sign the papers. Could I have stopped the sale by refusing to sign? T.H. had his way—as usual. The shooting increased incredibly. It seemed that they invited all of southwest Washington to come and share their rifle range. It seemed that people were camping out there. Theodore canvassed the neighborhood for names of people who would join us in suing the gun club for their unwelcome presence.

It seemed like this went on for years. We tried to buy back the place. We looked for another place to live. During this time, Sylvia had married Bud, and was living in Packwood. She decided to sell her timber. Bud was a fireman and didn't know anything about timber. Theodore must have been cruising the timber. They went up in the woods together for many days. They reluctantly joined our suit against the Gun Club. Some days were reasonably quiet, others unbearable. Anne gave me the key to her apartment downtown, so I often went there to escape. I think

Theodore enjoyed gadding about looking for another place for us to live. I didn't always go along. One day when I was working in my flowerbed, those jolting explosions began, and I ran crying aloud in anguish and despair to the house. Of course we did not win the case, but they did modify their shooting somewhat. It helped. Nobody camped there and left garbage again.

We managed to go to Latah once a year, and over to Bob and Ruth Pittman's in Yakima more often. One trip we went to Walla Walla and looked up the cousins there. Another time the cousins there had a family reunion. Susan came to spend a week with me every summer until she began having health problems. We did stop to see her at her apartment, on one trip. I enjoyed the Latah picnics on Memorial Day, when I would see old friends. One special 60th anniversary of my high school graduation class, I went over for Erma and Burl's fiftieth wedding anniversary. I sang *I Love You, Truly*, as I did the first time.

One Sunday in 1980, we decided to make our usual trip to Latah earlier than usual for some reason. It was the 18th of May. When we stopped in Castle Rock at a service station for gas, I heard an attendant say, "There's a wall of mud coming down the Toutle River." We went on our way casually, wondering what had happened. We stopped at the exit to highway 12, where we always went over White Pass, to telephone the State Patrol to find out if the road was open. The cars there at the service station had lots of ash on them. Mount St. Helens had been a source of interest for many months. We went north planning to go through Snoqualmie Pass instead. It was also mostly closed. We decided to stop in at Leona Schwartz' for a while before we started further north. It was near three o'clock when we decided to just go back home again. If we went for Latah now, we would have to go up the Columbia River Gorge, through Portland.

The State Patrol informed us that I-5 highway was closed. We would have to go west to the beach, and then come east again on the Columbia River Highway. As we were at the intersection ready to go to the coast, we saw traffic moving south again and were told that the Toutle River Bridge would be open until 4:00 p.m. After that time they expected another heavy flow of ash. We thought that we could make it, so we headed south. There before us was Mount St. Helens with that living plume of ash that you see on pictures now. We got across to Castle Rock, crossed over the Cowlitz, which was thick with mud and debris, then on toward home. Sylvia called up to find out if we got home safely. There were more minor eruptions. A week later, the wind blew from the northeast carrying another load of ash, darkening our sky one morning for a while and covering everything with ash. The grass was full of ash. I had to feed the sheep hay in the barn for a week or so until it rained enough to wash it off. Everything was dusty. The tent caterpillars were all apparently killed by the ash, because they were not seen again in the area. Many song birds were also victims.

Theodore didn't do any more real logging. He had a skidder now instead of a tractor. The TD-14 needed too much repair. I don't know how he used the skidder; but it made a lot of noise. He kept busy when he felt well. He enjoyed cutting firewood. He sold some, and gave some to various widows: Edna Howell, who lived toward the end of Ragland Road; Bertha Lawson, whose husband, Walt Rogers, had been our bookkeeper for most of his real logging years, (she was widowed again, as Archie Lawson also died); and Violet Pinxton, a colored lady who was Ted's next door neighbor on 8th Avenue, and still had his stove. Besides our own supply of wood, he had extra piled under the eaves of the garage. We also took pick-up loads of wood to Bob and Ruth Pittman in Yakima.

It was in the spring of 1981 that Theodore began to have chest pains occasionally. It seemed like indigestion, but we went to see Dr. Fritz for his opinion. After several visits there, he was sent to the Longview heart specialist, Dr. Neal Kirkpatrick, who said he had a leaking valve, and recommended a heart operation. We bought a new car that spring. It was the first new car we ever had. With it we took Theodore to the hospital in Portland. I was very confident that he would come through this safely. He was in good physical shape all of his life. He had quit smoking many years ago just like Archie, and was not overweight. Anne and I went to see him several times. She was better at driving in Portland than I was. Ted went into a different Portland hospital the same week to get his jaw re-set, so it was painfully wired in place and he could only eat liquids sipped through a straw. They somehow talked with each other by phone every day. They both fully recovered. I think that was the summer we sold the sheep, so there were no more barn chores for me, but I missed them, and one day I went over into Oregon to find them and see them again, but I couldn't find them. We must have bought more sheep later because they are mentioned in my diaries of later years.

Troy Laundry, where Ted was the washerman, closed. In the summer he packed his car and went to Sioux City, Iowa. I missed him, and wrote to him quite often. I don't know just when it happened, but it was a sunny day when I was doing the washing. As I was hanging up the clothes out on the porch, I thought I heard Theodore's voice down by the pond. He had gone down there sometime earlier, so I walked down the hill to see. I found him—not by the pond—but under a log that had rolled over on him while he was cutting wood. He said, "Take the Peavey and roll this log off of me!" I set the Peavey hook in the log knowing that if it slipped off, the log would probably finish rolling down and crush him to death right in front of me. It was frightening, but I did it just right. I took him in to the emergency room. He had a gash on his chin—not too bad—and I don't remember what else.

Sylvia, Bud, and Angie were living in Packwood. They came so often while she was having her timber logged. According to my diaries, it was June 1982 when Sylvia married Bud Kline and moved to Packwood. She was officially out of the clutches of Sal Carraba, the Sicilian saxophone player from south Seattle, a chain-smoking Musician's Union official whom T.H. referred to as "Old Lucifer." I hadn't heard from Cynthia for quite a while, and we got an invitation to her wedding in California to Danny Rodriguez.

During the following years, when Sylvia was having her timber logged, she had Maurice's old flute reconditioned, and it became Angie's instrument. She took lessons here, and she was a good player, and played with the local Youth Symphony. Our problem with the Gun Club dragged on for years, it seemed, and I was constantly taking medication for depression. I went to Anne's apartment to escape "battle fatigue." I went to our property on Puget Island and sat there thinking about having a house there, and doing my farming in peace and quiet.

That wasn't reasonable. At seventy years old, I should be thinking about retirement. Ted was in Iowa for a year to learn to tune and repair pianos. Anne had an operation in a Seattle hospital that year. She lived in Seattle in the late 1970's and was back in Longview now as a big wheel at the Longview Bon Marche. I remember giving her some plants for her place there. Now she was back, and living at a different apartment, where she became acquainted with Jaswant, the man she eventually married on April 19, 1984.

Theodore had another close call. It was the next year about noon one day when he decided to clean some moss off of the roof. I said, "No, no; you shouldn't do that." He was about eighty years old. Well, he did it anyway. I waited in the front room for the inevitable to happen. Sure enough, I heard a thud. I looked out the front room window to the west side. There he was lying on the ground. I got him to the hospital. They kept him there for several days. Doctor Neal Kirkpatrick called to say that he had a couple of cracked ribs and a slightly punctured lung. His appetite had returned, and he was being taken out of intensive care that morning. He sustained no lasting damage. He had lots of company. Sylvia and Bud came, Mister and I, Mrs. Clifton took flowers, Ted, Mervyn, Mr. and Mrs. Underhill. When Underhills left, he got hostile and quarrelsome, so we left, too. The nurse called to say they were having trouble with him. Then Ted called to say the same thing. Then T.H. called to tell me to pick him up at Mervyn's. The next day I took him back to the hospital for an enema. He sure needed it! Maybe that was why he was so bellicose. The NEXT day I took him to Kirkpatrick's office for a checkup, and he was doing just fine.

Maurice's children came and went, usually asking for money. Theodore was in charge of Maurice's estate. He gave up that job, and turned all the records over to Dave Hallin, our lawyer, for relief of any responsibility. There was no money left, but they kept asking for money anyway. Steve came to live with us one fall and go to high school. He stayed about three months. He was playing hooky because he was not interested and thought he already knew it all. He went back to Astoria and never did finish high school. Mister stayed with us about a week. He found out that he could have a part-time job at the fish cannery in Astoria, so he went there to work, and finished high school. I sent him money for the rent on his small apartment every month until he graduated. We tried to get him started in college. Ted had appointments set up for entrance, but he skipped out and went back to Astoria. They frequently came and went, often with friends. I think Theodore would slip them a few bills, especially Mister.

Countless times I sent money to Nina. Sometimes she would pay me back, when she was working. Once she sent me a picture of a little nine-year-old boy, Nathan. This was her baby that she brought to see me in May when she was fifteen years old. He was such a sweet baby, born on March 21st. I advised her to find someone to adopt that dear little one. She wouldn't possibly provide a good home for him. What kind of a home did she have with her mother? Ted had an extra bedroom at his place on 8th Ave., and had old Mrs. Pinxton next door lined up to watch the baby while Nina finished high school—if she wanted to take the responsibility herself. The wisest thing she did was to give him to Don and Dee Bartlett, the couple who had been her foster parents. He was our first great-grandchild, and I would never see him, or get to know him.

The doctor said that Theodore made a remarkable and complete recovery from his heart operation. Maybe it was old age that caused a gradual personality change. He was rather quarrelsome. He hated my driving. Once, on the way home from town, he wanted out of the car. I must have stopped at a red light at an intersection. He got out, and I went on home. I never did find out where he spent the night or how he got home. He began to have trouble with numbers. He would spend hours working on making out receipts for the income on the property we sold to the Gun Club. Finally he gave up, and I began doing it.

Sylvia's marriage to Bud Kline did not last long. She said that he was an alcoholic. She left him and went back to her home at Belfair. She was there when Cynthia came from California on a visit, bringing another great-grandchild, little Daniel. Ina went with me to Belfair to see them. Sylvia was a favorite with her. I signed up that fall for a class at the college—How to Manage Your Money. I enjoyed that class. My old friend Dr. John Nelson was there along with other pleasant people. I attended other lectures, or seminars, on the subject. I am a conservative investor. Interest was high, and I invested in municipal bonds. We had a good income, cutting coupons.

One weekend in July we went to Port Angeles. I don't know what the occasion was for a party. Maybe it was the twins' past birthday. Lucille was there. Ted and Angie came, and Sylvia—with a new friend, Jack Wasson. Anne did the chores so that I could stay overnight. We looked at the property that Lucille bought in Sequim for an investment. I thought it would be a good place to live. We stayed with Jerry and Carol overnight. Jack was from Randle. Sylvia met him while she was living in Packwood with Bud, but I don't know how. He grew up with his grandfather who was a brother to our Aunt Mathilda's husband, Uncle Jake, who lived in Chehalis. We used to stop and see them once in a while on our way to visit Theodore's folks. Uncle Jake was a great hunter, so Theodore found him interesting.

Susan had just gone home from her annual visit with us when we got a call from my uncle, Harold Harrington. He was coming to visit. He had been in Portland visiting his only son, Claude. My aunt, Helen, had died. He spent about a week with us; then we took him to Yakima. We stopped in Kelso for gas, and as we were leaving, T.H. had one of his temper tantrums over my driving. I was not driving off into the traffic fast enough to suit him. I finally got him back into the car, and we drove on in silence. When we got to Packwood, he wanted out rather than going along to Yakima. So, we left him there and went on. I spent a pleasant day with Bob, Ruth, and family. Harold stayed, and went from there to visit the relatives in eastern Washington, and from there on back home to the Mid-west. I went home, too. I got back to Packwood about five thirty. Theodore was on the street looking for me.

I don't know just what Ted was doing now. I think that he was living in an apartment downtown and working for Merv's wife at Robbins Bookshop. Robert Oman, his childhood friend, died of heart trouble in California before he could go to see him on his return from Iowa. In December we took a pick-up load of wood to Sylvia at Belfair. Ann was real disappointed when Jaswant, her husband, could not be with her at Christmas. It was January when she got word that he now was able to be here and would get here in about ten days. There was snow that winter which made it hard to travel, but we had company anyway. Sylvia and Jack came on his birthday (January 29th.)

A young man, Bob Webster, came and offered Theodore $300,000 for the place. Sylvia was afraid that he would just sell it immediately without knowing how much it was worth. The timber had not been cruised or anything. Nothing happened. It was a cold and snowy winter. Sometimes it was pleasant to walk out in the snow. It was quieter somehow. Gun Club people had trouble traveling, too. The Webster family came several times to see the place. Finally I told Websters that I didn't want to sell, and that T.H. could not sell it without my consent. It was not going to be another "Gun Club" transaction.

When spring came, now it was Jack and Sylvia who came to do her logging, and they found the place in Randle that she wanted to buy—Hampton House—a large, stately home built on the old highway by the lumber mill family. On our way back from the annual meeting at Latah in May, I drove by the place for Theodore to see it. Another time we went with them to see the inside of it. Somehow Sylvia raised the money to buy the place, except for a small amount. We co-signed the mortgage at Seafirst Bank. Maybe it was June when she moved in. I'm sure Anne went with me several times to see the place. Sylvia was turning it into a Bed & Breakfast; Anne helped with the advertising and gave her tips on interior decorating. We also took Ina with us on one trip to see the place and drive around the country there.

Theodore had divided the 80-acre Logan place over on Ragland road into two parcels, north forty and south forty. Fortunately, Ted got the south tract which adjoined his other property. Sylvia got the one on the road, which seemed the best at the time. Now Jack also had to take care of that property on their frequent visits to see us. Ted lived in town, but came out frequently. I think that it was that summer when T.H. watered my Double Delight rose with chainsaw fuel. It must have been in August, I asked him to pick the rest of the Yellow Transparent apples. They are the first to ripen, and then get mushy. The Yellow Transparent were one limb on a tree of grafts. He picked the northern Spy limb as well—knurly little green apples that would not have been ready until late October or November.

He seemed all right most of the time. One day after he and Jack had been cutting and wrapping meat for the freezer, he was worried. His arm and hand were so numb. We went to the hospital emergency to have him checked, and waited hours before they would see him. Next day I took him to the hospital, then to the doctor's office where they gave him a thorough exam and said that he made a good recovery from a light stroke.

My prognosis was not as good. It seems that I had some kind of blood disorder.

Ted lost his job at the bookshop, and went back to help at Longview Furniture Repair again. He was on and off there for years. He and Mike Bolin apprenticed there together, and Mike bought the shop; Ted went to Iowa, and then worked there at odd times. Sylvia wanted him to go to a psychiatrist in Yakima. He did not want to get fixed unless something was broken. He told her that if she thought that he was not in sound mind, to just go ahead and commit him to the mental department of the hospital. She and Jack came to town to see Ted—and did commit him to St. Johns Hospital where he spent the weekend being observed and answering their questions. Theodore was surprised, and went to see him there. Sylvia and Ted have never been the same since. He threatened to return to us all that we had ever given him and just go away. I couldn't bear to think of life without Ted. Thank God he is still here. Nobody came to take him away.

Sylvia and Jack came often, Stuart came once for wood. In all these past years we went often to see Sherm and Minnie Sterling in Chehalis. Now Sherm was gone. He and Minnie came home from church one Sunday in the spring. He said he did not feel very well and lay down for a while. His death was sudden, but peaceful. Theodore was the only one of his Sterling generation left. In the fall, we got word that Minnie was also gone. We went to Yakima to see Bob and Ruth, as their health was declining, too.

We had young friends, too. Paul and Betty Clark bought a piece of property from us on the Coal Creek Road between Clarence Young and the Allison/Wright houses. This was the legal access from Coal Creek

Road to our property. There was a road there that went right on the usual lot line for residence which we used for trucks hauling logs. The Clarks built a home on it for themselves, and came by faithfully every month to make a payment on the property. He was an expert auto mechanic who worked in a local garage. We would often have him work on our vehicles. They are such pleasant, Christian folks. They remembered our fiftieth wedding anniversary, and took us out to dinner. We enjoyed many musical evenings with the Clark extended family as they played guitars and sang inspirational songs.

In October of 1985, we were invited to John and Rose Paul's fiftieth wedding anniversary celebration at the Portland Airport. John's son was an airplane pilot. Lillian came and stayed overnight to join us. It was a gala affair. I was glad to see him and his family. I hoped that we could continue to be in touch with them, but it didn't happen. As with all of the Paul kids' children, we don't know any of them. Strangely I did contact the McCabes, our childhood playmates who moved away to Thornton, and then to Portland. One evening when I was alone watching the evening news on television, they were televising the retirement of the Portland Chief of Police, Vern McCabe. I wrote to him in care of the Police Department, and he answered. He told me about his family, and where his brother, Jack was and gave me his address. So I wrote to him also; and he answered, too. He had spent all of his life working for Continental Can Company, and was living in New Jersey.

Theodore went to see Kenny Peterson real often. Many of his old friends were disappearing. We never had better friends than Kenny and Leona. I wonder if they noticed his forgetfulness. He often had indigestion. He did not drink milk; it seemed to disagree with him. Strawberries gave him the hives if he had too many. Ted seemed to inherit that from him. He used dried papaya to help settle his stomach. I took him to the emergency room on several occasions. Once, when we couldn't get waited on, he just gave up and we went back home.

I had some good times with the church people at the Assembly. We went on trips together—once on a sightseeing trip to Seattle; another time we went to British Columbia. Lillian came over from Port Angeles to Victoria and spent a little time with us. We always had such a good time.

Anne was truly a part of my life as much as Sylvia was. We went places together. She dropped in often. We had girl-to-girl visits about her love affair with Jaswant. I missed her if she didn't drop in regularly. That happened when she got sick. They were living in a mobile home down by the Coal Creek Store when I went to see her—maybe with her mother, Ruth, who had also lived in the same mobile home before moving to Castle Rock. She was moved from there to a hospital in Seattle where she died that summer at 43 years of age. It didn't seem fair. I was old and tired of living. Her friends had a Memorial Service for her at the Coal Creek Church. Reza and her Iranian friends from Seattle brought a huge orange tuberous begonia. The Kemp boys stayed overnight with me. Kathy Jones played piano, Rick Kemp played trumpet, Mervyn Puvogel sang *And the Trumpet Shall Sound*, her favorite from the *Messiah*. The music was best because of Mervyn, and Ted. Bill Paxton did not show up. T.H. could not seem to understand quite what all the people were there for. He loved Anne, too; but he was confused, and stayed home. Both husbands, Reza and Jaswant, were gracious to each other. Obviously they both loved her. Upon her death she was cremated and scattered—her wish. After the service, Rick played *Amazing Grace* from the porch of the church. It made the valley echo on the clear, sunny day—now hollow. Life went on for the rest of us. Jaswant brought back the tulip quilt that I had given to Anne. Her family was taking care of the rest of her things. Jaswant said, "I'll load my things in my little car to go; and take Anne with me in my heart." So, I never saw him again. He lived in Seattle for a while, and then returned to Amritsar, India, where he was from. Life went on.

Lorna and her husband came that summer. I gave the tulip quilt to her. Ted came and went to dental school in Portland that fall. I know that I wanted him home more. Jack and his son, Brian were here for a few days every week taking care of Sylvia's timber. Reluctantly, Theodore finally arranged to have our hand-split cedar shake roof (that he split himself) replaced. It was beginning to leak. All those shakes had to be removed. Susan was with us that fall, and helped Ted pick them all up. He used them by turning them upside down and end for end to put a new roof on the old garage that Rube Sterling built, and also the chicken house.

It was before this in the late 1970's when T.H. was in better shape, that Ted lived in a place that he bought for himself in Acme, Washington. Theodore drove up there with the pick up on several occasions to help him fix the house and move there, then to move back to our place after a fire burned his house down in the winter. I've omitted some other important events. Jeannie's wedding at Poulsbo. Lu was there, Mom was there, everybody was there and we had a wonderful time. She married the original Norwegian bachelor, Harold Paulson, who came from there. I do not remember what year.

Sylvia had a great family reunion at her Hampton House in Randle. Everybody was there—Ross and Wyona from Moses Lake, Lu and Fritz and more. Just look at the pictures.

As Theodore's health deteriorated, I couldn't take him to Latah with me any more. Once I left him with Sylvia in Randle and I went on. The next morning a neighbor called Sylvia saying, "I think I see your father walking down the road. Check and see if he is there." Sure enough, he was going home. He often worried about Ted when he didn't get home on time. He imagined that he'd been robbed or had an accident. He would take the car and go to find him—not even knowing where to go. Maybe he just went off the road right here in the canyon like Hamid did. He had to go and see. Ted would play for a dance someplace on the weekends while he was going to dental school. He worked from Newport, Oregon to Raymond, Washington, and tried to spend at least one day here with us.

One day he left his antique 1948 Chevrolet pick-up parked at the bottom of the hill instead of in the old garage. When Theodore saw it he said, "It's not safe down there like that. I need to pull it up the hill here." So he took our pick-up down there to tow it up. The inevitable happened, as I expected it would. I heard a profound splash. Ted's green pick-up was out in the pond surrounded by muddied water. Theodore asked me if Ted would notice! I called up Jack. He and Brian came on Monday morning to pull it out. The next day, when Theodore saw it there, he had totally forgotten all about that episode, and wanted to get it up the hill again. I threatened to call the police if he did anything to that pick-up at all. It still had the displaced pond weeds clinging onto it.

He finally left it alone.

After I went to bed, he would stay up and explore. One night he took apart all of the framed pictures to see what was behind the pictures. What a mess. Ted gave us a mirror for the basement which had the back nailed on just so he could not molest it. Quarrelsome and unreasonable, Theodore became more and more difficult to live with. On one occasion I packed my overnight bag and went away to find a place where I could live alone. It would have to be small and cheap. I had very little money of my own. I was gone overnight. When I got back—about noon the next day—he was sitting in his rocking chair. The house was cold because there was no fire in the furnace. He had not had anything to eat. I could not leave him! Who would take care of him? He needed me, and that was my job, "in sickness and in health." One day he asked me if I was his mother. I said, "No, I am your wife."

It was in February of 1988 that Mister announced that they were selling the timber on their forty acres. When Mister came to talk to him about it, Theodore would only talk about something else. I insisted that the loggers maintain our road in good repair, and they did. By and by Theodore saw those loads of beautiful logs going by our house daily. Why wasn't he getting checks? He went to the lawyer, Hallin; he went to the Weyerhaeuser office to complain; he called the sheriff about timber theft. One day he stopped one of the truck drivers down by the Coal Creek Store. The man must have understood the problem, and took him along to deliver the load. He started a series of barricades across the road.

In April, Ted and I went to Paul Osterberg's wedding in Portland—his second marriage. He was Theodore's sister Esther's youngest grandson. It was a fun time. His little son, Andrew—such a cute little boy—asked me to dance. I never danced in my life. I think that his grandma, Melba, put a bug in his ear to do that. Melba and John, her second son, came the next Saturday to see us and she told me that I should put Theodore in a nursing home. Melba was a career nurse and worked for years at the military hospital in Vancouver. Susan was there that week and stayed with T.H. while we were gone.

Sylvia called one day saying that she had found a house there for me to look at. We went to Randle. Theodore liked to travel around even if he did not like my driving. It was a new double-wide mobile home on two and a half acres beside Silver brook, a nice little tributary of the Cowlitz. It was a lovely spot, ready to move into, and I wouldn't have to wait to develop the place that was in front of the Hampton House. So I bought the place. I went there every Wednesday to mow the lawn and plant the garden that spring. Theodore would want to go over to Sylvia's most of the time. Jack and Stuart moved some of my furniture–desk, davenport, and beds–so we could stay there overnight. We had company there. Lu and Fritz stopped by to see the place. Cynthia and her family camped out along the stream for several days. Cynthia agreed with me after that; camping out is *not fun*.

Finally I realized that Theodore would never stay there. I had to move back to Coal Creek again. We had several offers to buy the farm that summer. Bob Webster came back with an offer. IIe wanted it real bad. There were two other offers—and Maurice's children wanted to buy it with the money they had from the logs. What would they do with it? That was absurd! They would never live with us there on the place, and wouldn't know what to do with it. Should we give it to Sylvia and Ted? They were not speaking to each other. This would probably just give them another bone of contention.

We sold it to Scott Shulke. When I found out that I could not move T.H. away from there, I offered to sell just the west half. He said, No they did not want to move. His children wanted to stay in the Castle Rock School District. We could stay there as long as we wanted to. That clause must have been written into the contract. The Shulke family came into our lives from the Coal Creek Curch, where Floyd took on pinch-hit preaching. Floyd, Jean, and their family, Mike, Judy, Scott, and Joe lived on Delameter Valley Road. They had the farm of Mr. and Mrs. Percy Affleck, the parents of Jean. Floyd was a logger by trade and had done some logging for T.H. in the past. Scott was an upstanding Christian young man. He was in church every Sunday and taught a Sunday school class. He and his wife, Stephanie, had a daughter, Michael Ann, and a son, Justin. I was sure that I could depend on him to be fair and honest. He was younger, but a friend of Ted's. We went to Hallin's office to draw up the contract.

In the fall, Ted took a class in building construction at Lower Columbia College. Tom Satterlee was the instructor. As a class project, they began building a house for him on up the hill past ours on his place in the spring. I wanted him to let me build or help him build a house on his Woodside Drive property. He didn't want to. Since Scott was a heavy equipment operator, Ted hired him to do the excavation and preparatory work on the site, the septic tank drains, road, etc. and hauling lumber that he had milled for the project. On one occasion, the class arrived on the site only to find that Scott's work had not been done. He also installed the septic tank in the wrong place on purpose. Tom Satterlee was not happy with Scott because he was holding back the group effort, so Ted hired Laulinen to work for him instead, and re-install the septic tank where he wanted it. Ray was dependable. Ted had to do some logging on his place to pay for the construction in 1989.

Maurice's children each got about $70,000 from their timber. I told them that they should use the money to buy a home. Nina took my advice, and paid for a house that needed some repair. Her lover, John, who she had been traveling with and hoped to marry, was good at that. Apparently he didn't want the job, or her, and left. I found a nice, new small place on Coal Creek Road for Mister, but he was not sure that he wanted to live in Longview, so he didn't buy it. He never had a home. All that money went for rent—and other things I learned about much later. The same with Steve. After John left her Nina was heartbroken. She kept waiting and hoping that he would eventually come back. She got a job at Goodwill in Longview. Her boss apologized to Ted later for getting rid of her, but she would or could not follow instructions.

Back to Theodore and the farm. He was more tranquil now with the logging stopped. Sometimes when he couldn't sleep, he imagined robbers were lurking around. Dr. gave me some medication for that. It was hard to get him to shave and to take a bath. I got a stool to put in the bath tub for him to sit on, making it easier for me to give him a bath. One day when we were expecting company he decided to go to the barbershop in town and get shaved. It was about noon when he left. Our company came and spent the afternoon. They were ready to leave when he came back—still with all of his whiskers. It is amazing that with all of his mental deficiencies, he always drove the car safely and found his way home again.

Ted stayed with him that year so that I could go to Sylvia's for Thanksgiving. Usually I could take him with me when I went to Fred Meyers for groceries. He would sit on a chair or bench near the check-out and often find someone there to visit with. When he couldn't do that any more, someone had to stay at home with him while I took care of other business. Sylvia had his name in at a Morton nursing home. Yes, I was running a nursing home. One evening I was getting him ready for bed about nine o'clock. Somehow he slipped down on the floor beside the bed. He couldn't get up, and I could not lift him. I called up Paul Clark. He came over and lifted him into bed. The next morning I couldn't get him up. He was incontinent and had been for some time. Keeping him clean and dry was no small task. I kept coaxing him to try to get up. I would help him all that I could, but he just lay there. Finally, I called 911. The Fire Department came and took him on a stretcher to the hospital emergency room.

When I went to see him the next day, he thought that he was in jail, and lay there wondering how he was going to break out. He was put in the nursing home. I went there to see him every day, and urged him to eat to gain his strength back so that he could walk out of there and come home again. Seeing that he was getting thinner and weaker, I usually cried all the way home. He remembered Hamid when he came over from Hawaii at Christmastime and visited him. Other friends came, too. One day his back was turned toward me as I approached. He was calling, "Rosie." I came and put my arms around him. How many times had he called me when I wasn't there?

It was winter. Sometimes there was ice and snow making it too dangerous for me to drive to town. Ted would visit him after his building class every day. Somehow he very consistently became "Archie" for his dad during this time rather than being himself. When I did get there, he didn't know who I was. He would go to the bathroom and stay there until it was time for me to leave.

Oddly, his last days, he knew me. Sylvia came to see him too. He hadn't been eating and looked like a skeleton. The nurse telephoned me that week for a conference. She wanted to know if they should send him to the hospital. He couldn't sit up. His kidneys failed several days ago, and now he was bleeding from the rectum. I told her to do what she thought best. I sat with him all day and held his hand. When I talked with him, he answered, "Yes," or "No." Finally I had to leave. I kissed him goodbye and said, "If you are not here when I come back tomorrow, I'll find where you are and come to be with you." So it is. Some day I will be with him again.

Early the next morning the nurse called saying that he was gone. Ted went there. I needed to go and make arrangements with the funeral home to pick him up and take him away. After doing that, as I drove away toward home, I cried out aloud in the agony of despair and loneliness. I must have felt the same way that a child lost somewhere in a mall would feel with no family or familiar person around. Funeral arrangements had to be made according to his instructions. Ted ordered a cedar coffin like the one they did for Maurice. Melba came to try and make things easier for me. I notified the folks at Multnomah. Aldrich was to do the service. Everything went well—just as Theodore had wanted it. After the service, we all went to the Coal Creek Church for lunch and a visit before going home. Then I was busy with "thank-you" notes for a time. I carried on with my life visiting neighbors, working on my quilting projects, and remembering all of the good parts of our life together. I would time and again be overcome with grief and loneliness.

Anne Hillman and Jaswant Ratoul

(l-r) Hamid, RosaMae, and Rahman Abbasteh, in kitchen of new house

Part Five – Widowhood
(1990's)

---◆◆◆---

In the spring, I decided to go to my house in Randle for a while. Maybe that would be the best place for me to live. It was cold, rainy weather, and then I decided that I would rather live in my house in Longview again. So Sylvia and Jack moved all my furniture back to Longview again, and rented out my house there in Randle to a pair of newlyweds. Then, I just gave the property to Sylvia, and never went back there again. She eventually sold it to a young couple there.

My next job was to take care of Theodore's will at the lawyer's office. That was a much longer and more time-consuming job than you might think. To re-assess the property and divide the investments equally took nearly two years. T.H. would have been 86 years old this April birthday had he not died in February.

On March 21st, Nina called me up to say that it was Nathan's birthday, and he would be fifteen years old. She had sent me a picture of him when he was eight. Had so many years gone by already? I wonder what kind of person he is.

I stopped in at Sylvia's on my way to Yakima, and unloaded some things for her. Then I went on to see Bob and Ruth. Sherman and Ruth were there visiting them. We had such a good time singing together–like old times. Then I stopped at Sylvia's again on the way home.

I spent quite a bit of time with cousin, Leona Schwartz, in Chehalis.

She was alone, too. In June that year we went over to Spokane together on the bus, where Lu took us around to see all the relatives-especially the Oakesdale cousins–who we didn't always see regularly. I also went with her to the Strawberry Festival at the Grange in Chehalis. I went to Randle quite often to help Sylvia there. Sylvia took my old Lang wood-burning kitchen range that was in the basement at the farm. She put it in her house in Randle. I often went there to help her–mostly in the garden–and that wasn't much. At home at the farm on Coal Creek, I had my own garden to do. Scott and Stephanie often dropped in. Once they cleaned my chicken house out for me. Another time they stayed for dinner–just like family. He did some repair work on the house. There was a lot of activity going on up the hill at Ted's place. Ron Wohl was logging for him.

All the money from those logs was going into the building project– which I considered very extravagant. I worried about that. It did not help my frequent spells of depression and loneliness without T.H. I often went to Hallin, our lawyer, for advice. He was taking care of the estate. When I had an offer for the Puget Island property, he said, "No, do not take less." I just kept it.

I had to ask him about investments while he was dividing the estate. I was called for jury duty several times during those years, but was excused until I finally asked to be permanently excused because of my age. That was the end of that. Leona and Kenny Peterson had to sell their farm and live across the street from her daughter. Kenny was getting forgetful just like T.H. did. I went to see her there several times. Eventually Kenny had to be put into a nursing home. This was all too familiar to me.

There were wonderful family reunions at different times and places. One was at Jeannie and Harold's lovely new home in Poulsbo. Another time a reunion was called at the McMahone farm in Randle. That was a real big occasion. I picked up Leona in Chehalis when we went there. I met more relatives that I had never known of before at that reunion–and such food! Another was at Sylvia's Hampton House in Randle.

It was the summer of 1990. I sold the Puget Island property to the Hansens. Her parents lived on the Island, and this was going to be their permanent home. They became my good friends. I knitted an afghan for her baby, little Nels. Now and then I would stop in for a visit.

I thought that I would go and live with Sylvia when Ted got his house finished. She had asked me to. This was the plan until one day in August when Ted brought home the mail. There was the most hateful letter to me from Sylvia. It gave me a heart attack! She accused me of being partial and unfair. She thought that she should have the Puget Island property because she didn't get as much acreage as the boys. Apparently the mortgage that we paid off on the Hampton House and the property that I gave her on Silverbrook did not count. So! That is how my efforts to be fair turned out. We sold the farm thinking that we could divide the assets more evenly. I was in shock for days. That ended any more thoughts of living with her. I asked her to sign a document releasing her from my bank account. I did not go to Randle any more. The next time I went to see Leona in Chehalis, I told her that I would not ever be living in Randle. We visited a retirement home there, Woodland Estates. We thought that we might share a cottage. On a later visit we decided that it would be better to each have a small apartment in the main building. Each time we get calls from them, we tell them that we are not ready to come there yet.

I went to Lillian's more often. I showed her the letter! We shared problems, and pleasures. They had a Golden Wedding Anniversary celebration. They were considered long-time residents there in Clallam County, and it was written up in the local newspaper. Leslie Warwick saw it and called up Lillian. We met him at his house where we looked at pictures and remembered the Fairbanks School, and all of the friends and neighbors there. He had lived in Port Angeles for many years, too. Following is really Lillian's story. Johnny's deteriorating health was like that of T.H., and led to a nursing home, then finally to the grave. Ted got up at 4:30 on a Wednesday morning in November, and we arrived in Sequim at nine o'clock. Only the family was at the funeral home. We said a silent goodbye, and closed the casket, which was put in his vintage blue 1940 Chevrolet pick-up which he had bought new and had all those years, and Jerry drove him to the cemetery with only three cars fallowing. Carol's mother, Virginia, read some scripture; and we sang a few hymns accompanied by Carol on a little electric instrument. We attended a Memorial Service later at the church where they have many friends.

We went back to Lillian's house on our way home, where she had a lovely birthday cake for me. That was a total surprise. We got home again by eight o'clock. I lost another dear friend that month, Pete Scruggs. Other friends and relatives disappeared that year. Hamid's father, Jalal Jahanmir died in Arizona where he was living with Jamal, and was flown to Seattle for interment. Ted went there by train to be with the family. My aunt, Bessie, who always kept me up-to-date on the relatives in Minnesota was now gone. I have missed her up-dates ever since. Every year is like that. All of my old friends keep disappearing. I spend more time with those that are left. What are the options?

I joined the Community Choir. Mervyn Puvogel was the conductor, so I was not very worried about passing the audition for membership. I sang soprano. Here were a lot of younger people; and I always liked to sing. We did three concerts a year–fall, winter, and spring. I still have my long black skirt. Another class that I enjoyed one year at L.C.C. was How to Manage Your Money. We were supposed to learn how to invest for a balanced portfolio. My old friend, Dr. John Nelson was there, and other pleasant folks. John had a farm and also belonged to the Farm Forestry Association. I went with him and Maxine to Farm Foresters' Dinners in the spring where I met others. I invited Scott and Stephanie to go several times, but they never would. I don't know when John retired from being a physician. I know he is one year younger than I am–and we both like farms and farming. He took moving pictures of me on my farm and shared some others of his farms in eastern Washington. One was the farm that Bob Pittman once farmed for his dad.

Several years passed before Mr. Hallin finally had all of the information he needed to divide the estate. I became impatient with him. I wanted to put my half into a trust with Multnomah, like we had before. Nelson Repsold took care of that for me; and it was because of him that I became acquainted with Dale Hadley, who was my financial advisor for several years. It was September of 1993 when I first got my quarterly income from Theodore's half of the estate.

Although the 1990's were mingled with the many incidents of worry and distress that Scott constantly and intentionally caused or inflicted on me, there were also many pleasant and interesting events as well. I spent a week or so with Lu at their winter home in Arizona. Another time Lillian went there with me. We had such a good time! We met pleasant people. One friend, Doreen Angus, lives in Victoria, British Columbia, just across the Strait of Juan de Fuca from Lillian. I went to Bainbridge Island and spent happy times with the grandchildren here. They often came to visit me. Sharon and Marty Erickson stopped by every spring on their way north when they were traveling for HCJB, the missionary organization that they were working for when they lived in Quito, Ecuador. They liked to spend time on our farm.

I've mentioned some of the family reunions. In the summer of 1993 was the biggest one of all. I drove to Bainbridge Island. From there Stuart & Laurie, Lauren, and I flew from the Seattle Airport to Minneapolis, where we met Lorna, who came from her place in Michigan. I think we went by bus south to Waterville, the nearest town to where the Pittman family met. There were hundreds of people there–cousins that I had not seen since childhood. Many came from far and near that I didn't even know. Someone had drawn a diagram of the family tree, and we all could find where we fit in. We took a trip over to Kilkenny to see my grandfather's farm, which was now occupied by his grandson. The school and other places that I remembered from my childhood were looking somewhat different now. So was I. There was a lot of corn.

I drove over to Spokane and Latah on many occasions–Mom's 90th birthday party, Erma and Burl's 60th wedding anniversary. Again, I sang *I Love You Truly*, as I had done originally. There was also the Fairbanks School reunion. That was where I went to school until the eighth grade. There were so few of us left–and now we were old and had to introduce ourselves. I often stopped at Moses Lake to see Ross and Wyona Sterling. I finally went there for her funeral. It was there that I met Lucille and went on with her to Spokane for a while to see her new home at the retirement place.

By far the most interesting trip was to Ecuador with Sharon (Williams) and Marty Erickson, who had lived there as missionaries for

HCJB for years. We were welcomed at the airport in Quito by our good friends, the Rojas family. We visited the HCJB radio station, since that was their purpose in being there–to broadcast the Bible. We had rooms in a facility provided mainly for missionaries passing through.

They also have a hospital there, and own property at a place called "Shell" some miles away from Quito. The poor roads made that trip quite exciting. More details of that trip are with the pictures. I bought two nice sweaters at a market there. Since I do not speak Spanish fluently, Marty did all of the negotiating for me. More details with my packet of pictures. On June 6, 1997 I was back home again. Mingled with all of the pleasant times with family and friends, were many losses–neighbors, friends, and relatives.

Another real pleasant time was when I shared the girls' (Lillian and Lu) 80th birthday celebration. We boarded a cruise ship in Seattle, and sailed up Puget Sound to Friday Harbor where we spent the night. The next day we sailed on to Victoria, B.C., Canada. We met a friend there– Doreen Angus. We had lunch with her and spent some time exploring the city and visiting her apartment until time to board the ferry to Port Angeles. Jerry was there at the dock to take us home to Lillian's house where we were surprised by other family members singing "Happy Birthday." There was a big cake, too. I think this was the time Jerry took me home the next day in his airplane. I think Lu went along for the ride. It was such an interesting trip! We went low enough so that we could see and try to identify the area below us as we passed it. We saw Ted's farm from the air. That was certainly the quickest trip I ever made from Lillian's to home!

Even after Ted's house was finished, he still shared time with me. Usually he came down the hill to my house for dinner and to use the telephone. His house did not have electricity or a telephone. We went places together–to Dr. Hong, the acupuncturist in Portland. We also had season tickets to the opera in Portland. The summer that I got back from Ecuador, my knees hurt me so badly that I walked with crutches. He took me to a knee specialist at Providence Hospital in Portland who was recommended by Jim Clevenger. I decided that I should prepare for knee surgery in the fall and I would have all winter to recover. The doctor said because of my age, recovery would be very slow, and we should try cortisone shots at intervals. He had treated another patient this way quite successfully. So it was. After my shot I walked out of there forgetting my crutches I was so without pain.

It was January 1994 when I joined the Tai-Chi class. It is really good exercise. Several weeks later I caught cold. I thought that I was better, and I spent the afternoon with my friend Esther Dower. Dowers lived in the same block as Dr. Davis when I was there. My cold got worse. I finally took George Kilen's advice and had Steve take me to Kirkpatrick's office. He sent me straight to the hospital where I stayed until the following Tuesday–with pneumonia. Sylvia was here when I came home again, but she left on Thursday when Cynthia came to stay with me until Saturday of the following week. Then she took me to stay with my sister, Lillian, for two weeks. It's amazing how fast pneumonia ruins a person. I was so skinny and weak! I rested a lot in Lillian's new home. Stuart brought me home again when I thought that I could manage alone. I still had to rest a lot.

It must have been after Ted finished building his house and was re-foresting his land, that we became acquainted with Jose Rangel. He was a tree planter, and we became involved with him and tried to help him with his problems. He and his American wife, Trudy, lived in Ted's house briefly. We took him to eastern Oregon for a court appearance–it must have had something to do with his green card. Whatever it was got dismissed. The trip was so interesting. I had never been to Ontario or Vail, Oregon before. I really enjoyed it! We were friends with Jose for several years and tried to help his dismal situation.

Ted accompanied the voice class that Merv taught at Lower Columbia College. Since he was going in anyway, and they needed another person to make the class sail, I took it. It was there that I met Marina Santamaria who was new in town. She came to Longview when she retired to be near her daughter, Rebecca, who had three children. Marina lived in southern California for years where she worked in a hospital. She was a native of El Salvador, and a soprano. She liked to sing with Ted. Maybe she got him to start attending Spanish Church in Kelso where she often sang with him accompanying her.

They also performed regularly in Ilwaco at an outreach Spanish church there. She became my dearest friend. I sang songs with her in Spanish. Iglesia (Spanish Church) met on Sunday afternoons where we met more good people, Sigifredo Castro and his little boy, Alejandro (who was a student of Merv the rest of the week at the junior high school;) it was also here that we met the Bautista brothers, Carlos and Mario. I can not include the story of Mario's life. Suffice it to say, that he will always be our dear friend–even though he had to go back to Guatemala where he came from. He played guitar by ear; and Ted taught him to read music. He calls me "Mother;" and we hear from him regularly. The Castro family are our other Mexican friends. The difficulties she endured over the years to be here legally with her four children seemed endless.

Another person that Ted tried to help was C.J. Bowker, a Sioux Indian who he met on the Reservation as he came home from Iowa. I don't know the story on that, it's Ted's. C.J. and his three children lived in Ted's house for a time after Trudy, Jose, and family were gone. To help solve Rosa's problems with immigration, she divorced her husband, Sigifredo, and we witnessed her marriage to C.J. before Judge Altenhoff. It was totally a financial and legal arrangement, as they never did live together. She had a job and somehow shared her income with him. He took advantage of the situation–always asking her for more money. He turned out to be a drunken cull; no one could change that. At last she got a divorce after she acquired legal citizenship for her four children. The whole family is now legal and in a home they bought new in Longview. They have remained our friends.

Back to October 31, 1994; it was the day Leona Clifton took me to the hospital for a major operation. All went well. I had lots of company while I was there. Lillian came to stay with me when I came home; friends and neighbors came–sometimes bringing food to help. Scott came one dark and stormy night with a friend (witness) and demanded that I remove the car from the old garage in the pouring rain. Lillian's car was in that garage at the time. I asked her to move it; I didn't feel strong enough. Then he nailed a plank across the entrance. I called up Hallin the next day about it. He said to just rip the plank off and use it anyway, and so I did–until one day I came home and found it full of discarded machinery which he apparently installed with his backhoe. It was much too heavy for me to move, so it became a garbage dump.

It was March 21, 1993, the first day of spring, that I met the Bartlett family and Nathan, Maurice's grandson. He had those sparkly blue eyes like Maurice. In fact he looks very much like Maurice. Don and Dee's other two children came too. We had dinner together at the Monticello Hotel where Ted was playing piano in the dining room, so he met them too. Then we came home here to visit a bit before they went home again to the Oregon panhandle. I think my next encounter with them was when Nathan graduated from high school. I was invited to a dinner at their home after church one Sunday. I got there early enough to attend the service, and then I followed them home to where Dee had a dinner for all of the grandparents. It was a splendid afternoon. She showed me albums of pictures of Nathan's childhood.

He was certainly fortunate to grow up in a stable Christian home. I always try to remember his birthday and send him a card ever since. He stopped to see me occasionally when he was in Longview. On December 24, 1997, he came to my house by nine A.M. and we left for Bainbridge Island to spend Christmas with the grandchildren there. I stayed overnight at Stuart and Laurie's; and Nathan spent the night at Cynthia's. We left for home in the afternoon; Nathan drove. It was almost like having Maurice back for a while again. I bought myself a television for Christmas.

It was January 14, 1998 when Lu called up to tell me that Mom passed away. She just didn't wake up that morning. In the spring there was a Memorial Service in Latah. I saw cousins there that I had not seen for years and will probably never see again.

Lillian had surgery in February. When she came home from the hospital, I went to Port Angeles to be with her and help even though I am not a good nurse. When it was March again and time for Nathan's birthday, both Dee and I wrote to Nina asking her to transfer her 40 acres over to Nathan. She said that she had given it to Debbie Mathews. That was quite a shock to me! We continue to share good times with the Bartletts. Ted and I were there for Nathan and Heidi's wedding. Nathan and Heidi came to Jeannie's in Poulsbo for a Mother's Day party for me. The next spring I was in Bellingham when their baby, Logan, came–late in July of 2001. They brought him to see us after Thanksgiving that year. The following summer we drove down there to see them and their new country home.

Nina's health deteriorated to the point that she could no longer work. Her log money was gone; and she would have to go on welfare. She wanted to turn over her forty acres to her son, Nathan, who was now a teenager, not old enough to handle it wisely. Scott bought her forty acres for $2500 with the understanding that she could buy it back for the same price when she wished or got well. It never seemed like a good arrangement to me at the time, though I never did see the written contract. I was a trusting soul. That forty-acre-tract became a real problem.

The powerline road went across that property to Ted's place, and Theodore had forgotten to give Ted a written right-of-way through it, as it had always been used for access. Scott ripped out all of the property line markers and corners that we had established on that place. Then he told Ted that his buildings were on that 40-acre piece rather than his own place. I hired Roger Munson, a licensed surveyor, to establish the corners and have them legally recorded. That kept Scott in place, but not his cows.

My friendly relationship with the Shulke family began to deteriorate during the nineties. Stephanie got a job in town and was not interested in gardening any more. I still had plenty to share even though their cows got in it a few times and did some damage. Ted came down from his place every evening to share dinner with me; and each time encountered that electric wire which was put up across the road and invisible at night. It was supposed to keep the cows from going up to Ted's place, but it never did. They found plenty of other places to go past it and torment him. They brought me wood as was agreed, so Ted saw to it that I didn't run out. One year some wood that Shulke brought was not dry and it made my basement real damp and all the windows sweated with steam. When he came one very rainy day with another load, I told him not to put it in the basement; just to dump it outside. He didn't do that; he hauled it away. Maybe that was the last time he ever brought me any wood.

The road was another bone of contention. I once thought it would be helpful to share in its maintenance, and hired Laulinen to put a load of gravel on a bare place and dig the ditch a bit as I had often done. Scott chased him off for trespassing. I talked to Scott about that, and told him what I thought–that he was being pretty childish. He would not raise and lower the water level in the dam. The splashboard needed to be raised in the winter to let out more water and flush out the mud. Then it needed to be lowered again to hold more water during the summer and fall. One time the pond was running over the road and neighbors came and helped me raise the splashboard in the spillway.

There was a culvert at the corner of the road at the lower garden that was plugged up. I tried to clean it out with a shovel, but just didn't have the strength. Another rainy day, I saw Scott stop in his pick-up and watch the water pouring across the road. I thought that now he could see the problem and dig out that culvert with his backhoe. Wrong. He never did a thing, so one day I asked Ray Mellis, who was doing some work for Ted with a backhoe, to come down and dig out the end of the culvert so the water would go through it. It would only take a few minutes, so he did. Just as he was leaving, Scott came and began screaming at him for trespassing.

I had an interesting visitor this summer–Mooky Kim, from Korea. He had become Ted's friend when they were going to dental school together in Portland. When his wife came home from visiting her family in Korea, he brought her with their little baby, to come and see us too. She could not speak a word of English. They were so proud of that baby. She demonstrated the way Korean mothers rock their babies.

Another time, I came home from somewhere and Ted was talking to a lawyer about a lawsuit with Scott over some cedar logs that Ted had taken to the mill to be sawn into shingles for his house. What a surprise! T.H. had brought those logs to our place and stored them there expecting that we would someday need to replace the shakes on the house roof. They had been replaced with composition shingles. The lawyer told Scott that those logs and the pile of scrap metal and iron that I sold were not his unless it was specifically designated in his contract. Of course, it wasn't. The same was with the logging equipment. Scott bought the skidder on time payments. Scott came by later and apologized for getting mad over it.

Our contract read that the timber would be harvested by mutual agreement. One quarter I wrote to him not to do any more logging. He totally ignored my request. I complained about the alder that he was wasting. I couldn't even have someone get it for firewood for me. Another time when I asked him to quit logging he answered the letter saying that he would do it anyway. Since he was so difficult over sharing the road and the logging, I asked to buy back the 40-acre-tract. I went to Nina and asked her to let me buy back her forty acres. At last when the document was read, I took her over to Hallin's office to sign, and she did; but she seemed confused thinking Sylvia had something to do with this. I assured her that Sylvia didn't know a thing about it. It was some weeks later that the lawyer sent word to Scott that the money for the forty acres was there waiting for him to relinquish the property. Scott ignored the request and that money was there available for a year or more. I think he went to see Nina about it and gave her a bad time. She called me up and screamed at me for asking her to sign that paper.

Mingled with all these pleasant times I had in other places with friends was continuing harassment from Shulke. I tried desperately to buy back the whole place since there were so many complaints. That didn't work. I once asked my lawyer if it wasn't reasonable or lawful to expect a certain amount of land to be included with a rented residence on country property so I could demand that Shulke keep his cows out of my yard and garden. That didn't work. After he filled my garage with junk, he parked some old dead vehicle on the road around the garden that Ted and I used to come and go from my house to his. Shulke put gates across the main road–something that we had never done. He seemed offended when I asked him to keep his cows off of Ted's place. The gates did not control the cows. I dreaded seeing him walk up the road to my house. Sometimes I would get panic attacks just wondering what he was up to now.

Steve and Mister decided to harvest the timber on their seventy acres. It adjoined Ted's property on the north and east. The logs from the north end of the property were being shipped out on Stewart Road, so Shulke tried to stop that. One day a load of logs came down the road and found the gate locked. Someone came from the logging site with heavy machinery and set the gate aside. Think of the work time lost by all the workers! The third time that happened, the gate was demolished, and often Shulke screamed protests as trucks went by, but the logging got done. I don't know how much money the kids got for that timber; but I do know that they left some bills unpaid. A business that gave them credit because the Sterlings they had dealt with in the past had always paid their bills. During this time I kept trying to recover Nina's forty acres with Steve's help. It didn't work. Shulke must have gone to threaten her some way. She sounded so distressed.

The boys got their logs to market, but that was not the end of the trouble. Ted usually stopped at my house on his way home from town. On this particular evening, he left my house about nine o'clock. He was soon back again to use the telephone. The cows were in his yard again destroying his landscaping. He called the sheriff. He called the humane society to please remove those cows. He did not want Shulke on his property. The sheriff came out. They called Shulke to come and get the cows against Ted's request, and took Ted to jail on a criminal felony charge. I did not find this out until the next day when he was not around. They did Shulke a favor by issuing a restraining order so Ted could not come to my place.

We had to engage another lawyer who got him out of jail after 10 days. I went to see him in jail once with Jim Clevenger. He telephoned me when he got out, and I took him home up Ragland Road. Ted put a road through the Dietz place there and connected it to the other roads. Suddenly it was his only access. It was a steep, narrow, crooked road, but passable and was rocked. I left him off at the gate to that road and he walked in the rest of the way. Other days I drove there with mail, food, and supplies. He asked Ron Wohl to harvest some more of his timber so there would be money to pay the lawyers. For three days loads of logs came down the hill past my house where Shulke had his herd of cows enclosed in my yard with two gates. The loggers had to open and close each gate as they drove through. After the last load went by in the evening, Shulke would drive the cows out of there until the next morning. I was impressed when one of Ted's friends called to see if I needed any help, since Ted could never be there.

The felony charges were dismissed. The telephone conversation with Ted calling for help with the cows was lost and then found later and played. They said that they were going to slap him around a little bit while Ted was on hold. The judge saw it Ted's way. I decided that I did not have one real friend at the Coal Creek Church. My real friends were also Ted's–George Kilen, Gary, the Clevengers. We had to go to court again to defend Ted's right to use Stewart Road to his house. This began in October. The interviewing many witnesses and preparing for the court trial continued through the winter and to April when we finally went to court very well prepared, and won. Actually one of Shulke's witnesses helped our side more than his. The next time he went to small claims court to demand payment from Ted for work that he had done on the road. He lost that case too. Ted had never hired him to do anything. He was found out telling a lie in court by previous papers which caught him changing his story.

There was a time when Sylvia and Jack were concerned with my logging contract and wanted an experienced lawyer they knew in Centralia to look at it. Maybe he could and would give us some helpful advice. There was really nothing to be done to change things; but after they had a conference with the lawyer they asked Scott to brand the logs. Jack gave him a log-branding hammer. It made no difference, he never used it anyway. There was just no way that we could be sure that he was not stealing logs. Ted and I followed him to Weyerhaeuser and took pictures of his load of logs without any brands. It was simply not possible to always be there to watch every load that went out. Finally when the time had expired on the contract and the logging had not been finished, what should we do? Obvious options were to extend the time, or ask for payment on the balance. Sylvia and Jack seemed to think it best to ask for payment on the balance and be done with him. I agreed.

After the logging was done, I paid rent to live there–hoping that Ted would get electricity to his place and I could eventually live there. He had his house wired, but there was no electricity to his house. We were sharing everything anyway. He kept my lawn mowed in spite of Shulke, and saw to it that I had plenty of wood for the furnace. One year Shulke–pretending to improve the fence around my garden to keep his cows out–put a post in the middle of the gateway so that I could never get anyone to drive through it and plow it up in the spring. On the east side of the garden out of my sight from by yard was a convenient opening for the cows to enter. No more gardens there. I helped Ted with his nice, big garden up at his place, and we had lots of vegetables plus irrigation water taps on three sides of it.

The road was a never-ending problem. Once when the portion across Nina's forty acres became high-centered, Ted had Frank Mellis scrape it down. Again he was accused of trespassing. Shulke put a cow-catcher on the road at the property line between Nina and Ted. It was a good idea in theory, but it was never properly installed, so the cows just went around it. They were a constant threat because they were always hungry. Larry Wilson sold Schulke a bull that he had raised as a calf. It was fat and in great shape when he got it. After a year or so you would not have recognized it. The cows were fed better than the bull. They all had a miserable existence.

Another incident with the road happened in February of 1996 when heavy rain and melting snow caused flooding everywhere. I had to go to town on an important errand. I found water pouring over the road because the culvert was plugged. It was a spot where the road had been completely washed away years before. I hurried home hoping the road would still be there to go across. I was told to first call Shulke. There was no answer. It must have been late in the day when Ted came home. Seeing the problem, he began immediately to save the road. He called Frank Mellis to come and help him. Shulke must have come and found them there. Before long I saw two police cars turning around at the bottom of the hill. Oh my! Are they taking Ted off to jail again? No. He and Frank saved the road and cleaned out the ditches.

Since he couldn't have them arrested, Shulke got another longer culvert to be put in. He wanted to sue Ted for trespassing because he mowed my lawn. After his other experiences in court, he must have decided that it was not worth it.

It was June of 1997 when I got a letter from Steve saying that he was living with his uncle, Jimmy Mason, in Everett. He was in a program to recover from alcoholism. The next day, Nina and Mister came in the evening to tell us that Steven was dead. He died of an overdose of black tar heroin in the men's room of a Chinese restaurant there. Now we had to arrange for another funeral. We had lots at Bunker Hill. He could be buried beside his father. No! His friends wanted to have him buried in a Portland cemetery. Of course, they needed money. I gave them $500 and a piece of my mind. I reminded them–especially Nina–how they never would help me when I needed help. We attended the funeral in Kelso on the following Saturday and met a lot of his old friends.

Taking care of the income from the logs and the property wisely was another responsibility. When I went to the folks at Multnomah to renew the trust, Repsold, the lawyer, said that I was doing very well, but if I wanted help, he recommended Dale Hadley. I met with him every spring. We would have lunch together and go over my accounts. I don't remember any particular advice he gave me. I went to Ted's accountant, Carson Breland, to do my taxes instead of Hallin–who never helped me with anything. My income taxes seemed too much. The log money I put in annuity for Sylvia and Ted. But when we got paid for the balance of the timber, how should we handle that wisely? It should be invested where we could get continuing income.

For some reason about that time, I began wondering if I should have nursing home insurance. I called an insurance company. The response was surprising. I had three callers at the appointed time: the insurance man; a very pleasant woman, Kay Dalhe, who took care of estates; and another young man who may help my income tax problem. That was how I met Mike Chamness. He had analyzed my accounts and recommended how to handle the log money. We'll wait and talk to Carson Breland. Weeks passed. Finally he had some papers for me to sign, and he took me out to dinner. It had been a long time since any gentleman ever took me out to dinner; and he was such a pleasant person to be with. The next day or two I worried. Had I been charmed by this young man? Would he take all of my money and disappear? Old ladies had sometimes been fooled that way, and were too embarrassed to admit it. We shared many lunches and dinners. Mike is truly a dearest friend. His brokerage firm takes care of my accounts, and Dale Hadley was dismissed long ago. I do have one account at W.M. that I have always taken care of myself.

After Steve was gone, I went to the Cowlitz County Courthouse to see if the taxes were paid on the seventy acres. Of course, they were not. I paid one year taxes to keep it from being sold. Then I went to a lawyer to see if there was any way that I could get possession of it again. No. Possession would go to his mother. We would have to go to her for an easement to put electricity through to Ted's place. We hoped that would be possible. In the meantime, something had to be done about the road through Nina's forty acres. In his own slimy way, Shulke was taking steps to force Ted to use the Ragland Road access exclusively. Ted talked to the Eric and Willard Evenson about the problem. The Evensons owned the 169-acre parcel that adjoined our property just east of the barn and stretched northward just east of Nina's forty acres, and also just east of Ted's. Ted saw to it that Evensons had a written right of way through our home place. The grade of the road was too steep going up to Nina's. Ted proposed putting in a new road which would eliminate the grade problem, and the problem with Nina and Shulke. The road would go through the Evenson property exclusively and then come into Ted's place directly.

Eric came with his boys and looked at the situation. He said to me, "I wish that I could have bought your place." Oh, so do I! They made a written agreement with Ted which allowed him to build a road through the young forest trees and inherent blackberry bushes and bypass Nina and Shulke. In the process the existing road from Evensons to the Nina/Shulke forty-acre tract would be obliterated.

Since Nina and Shulke did not have a reciprocity clause allowing the 40-acres to use the Evenson road, technically they did not have anything to lose. It was a real chore to cut a trail through the thick brush with a chain saw holding grade and direction, but it got done. Ron Wohl got the project started from Ted's end, and yarded in all of the trees from the road construction into a cold deck pile there. All of the small tops and non-merchantable trees became my winter wood supply. As the work progressed, Evenson brought a truckload of culverts to put in the canyons. Willard said, "I've never met Shulke. I don't expect I ever will because I plan to go to Heaven."

Ted already paid a considerable amount of money to the P.U.D. to extend the electric line to his house. The P.U.D. needed to use the Stewart Road access to haul in their equipment. The Ragland Road access was too steep and narrow. No! Shulke would not give them permission. I tried one more time to get the forty acres before we started building the road. I offered to pay her $35,000. She simply ignored my request. We were well on the way building the road before Shulke found out about it. Then all of a sudden it was okay to use the existing road through the 40 acres. Suddenly the new road was finished and the access to the 40 acres was destroyed. Bonneville could use the road, but not Shulke. Of course it was rocked, ditched and had tum-outs for passing. It must have cost at least $100,000 to build that road. That was my reward for all the time and money I spent for helping Nina.

Even though Mister had sold his interest in the 70 acres to Steve, after Steve was gone, he asked Ron to take out the very last marketable timber. I think he left still owing Ron some for the work he had done. Much later–a gloomy, rainy day in January–Mister came to see me. He was crying and embarrassed to tell me that he had gambled away all of his money and spent time in jail for possessing drugs. I did not give him any money at this time–nor will I again. That ends my association with the family of Maurice. Nathan is a different case entirely.

Since I was expecting to move in with Ted as soon as there was electricity, I bought a recliner chair and had it delivered there. Ted had the circular 2-piece sectional sofa re-upholstered. I was sharing all the gardening, so I bought a green-house and had it delivered up there too. It was something that I had always wanted. I enjoyed it that year.

In the fall Ted began looking for a buyer for his place. There was too much work there for him to do, and he had health problems that I was not aware of. He never complained. Along with that, of course, was the question–where to live? I would have to move too. I think he first considered Ashland, Oregon, but was advised not to move to Oregon. I went with him on a trip to Walla Walla to look at potential places that he found at Dayton. I think that he wanted to be closer to a college. Nothing was available in Waitsburg. It was a very disappointing trip. It must have been in January or February when he sold his place and was given a month or two to move out. Then he was really busy looking for a place to live. Sometimes I went with him, but mostly he went alone.

When he found the place in Bellingham, it was very old and needed a lot of repair and remodeling before we could move in. He moved all of his things down into my house when his time was up. I gave my treasured grand piano to Ericksons and shipped it off to California, and still I had three pianos in my living room, along with my furniture. There was more stuff in the basement to sort out, give away, or sell. Months dragged by hoping every day that I could soon move out of there. Our friend, Sue Hinshaw, the voice teacher that Ted played accompaniments for gave us a great going away party. I hoped that Larry Wilson could take my green-house, but it was too hard to move.

Jack came and took the guns and ammunition. I think he took the meat grinder, and maybe other tools or logging equipment. He got the log-loading crane long ago. I wondered where I could find a new home for my one goose that was left. Her partner was found dead recently. She depended on the wild ducks that often flew in and helped to eat her food. I thought Ted would have to help me catch her. It was the very day before the movers were coming to strip the house. I looked out of the kitchen window, and there was that goose walking up the driveway past the dogs. She walked around the garage and sat down by the back door. I opened the trunk of my car, went around there, and picked her up. She was in a corner. I put her in the trunk and took her to town to the lake where she could live with other geese and ducks. I never had a chance to go back and see if she was doing alright. I doubt that she got fed as well.

Ted must have come on the train that day. The next morning I put my clothes and Tweetie, the canary, in the car. I went back to my bedroom for a coat and the movers had already put it in a wardrobe, so I grabbed another in the utility room as I went by. Ted loaded the pick-up with gardening tools, the dogs, Chumley and Spooky, the skittish black cat, Snowflake, and I don't know what else, and we left that place forever.

Cynthia Holmes and her adopted
brother, Scott, in California

RosaMae & Marina Santamaria (r) on bus trip to Ilwaco

Part Six – Off of the Farm
(2000's)

———◆◆◆———

We both drove down Stewart Creek Road that last time separately and at different times in different vehicles. Ted stayed behind with the movers. I drove to Bainbridge Island, and stayed there until Sunday when Cynthia brought me home to Bellingham. While I was there, Sylvia had a birthday party for me over in Poulsbo where she lived in a condominium. It was November of 2000; I was turning ninety years old.

Cynthia unpacked most of the kitchen things before she went back home on the train. There was still much work to be done on the house, but we could eat and sleep there, and it was warm. There was too much furniture for that house. We found a place to sell it. Bill Faust, the contractor working on the house brought their new baby boy, Asa, over with him one day to show him off. I got to hold him for quite a while– until Bill came back from an errand. Bill and Rachel were our new friends. Little by little we found others. Sandra Peterson, the realtor, who was Ted's agent buying the place came by to see how I fit into the house, too. I met her mother, Florence, who lived with her, and became friends.

Robin Felper was our interior decorator. He was romantically involved with Sandra Peterson; but they did not live together. He lived on Lummi Island out in Bellingham Bay. He took us to another house that he was working on for ideas that might work for us. It was a big, old house–probably a hundred years or more–sometimes called "the Castle". It belonged to Edward Davidson, who also became our friend. He spent roughly nine million dollars on real estate in Bellingham; he was from San Francisco, but had not been in town too many years himself. Also through Robin, we met Charlie Henson, a retired history teacher also from the Bay Area, who was another client of Robin. Somehow we all got to know each other. Charlie invited us to a party at his house which he threw for Tom, who was a U.S. Ambassador who was being transferred from perhaps Egypt to India.

We went to Edward's parties on Labor Day. This was an outdoor event. He also had Halloween Parties with interesting costumes, and some sort of Christmas Party, which I preferred to the Halloween parties. He also had New Year's Eve parties. Usually live music was involved. He loved to give tours through the house and show off his relics.

Our friends across Jersey Street from us (cattycorner) were Shirley and Milton Moldenhauer. He acted like the unofficial mayor of Jersey Street. He told us not to get rid of the big Monterrey Pine tree in the front yard, and loaned tools during the remodel. Shirley was a landscape painter. They had a big garden. She brought me raspberries and odd vegetables. We visited for hours about our lives on farms. They were retired dairy people. Milton became more and more incapacitated with back trouble. Sometimes Shirley would come over and play Scrabble with us. She also made wine. When the temperature got over about sixty degrees, she complained about being too hot and was all flushed. It was a standing joke.

I found a full-gospel church, where I met many friendly people. They had a bus come and pick up those of us who had no transportation. I did drive in Bellingham, but the church was quite a way, too far. I could drive down the hill to my hairdresser, at the Leopold Hotel. My bank was in that block, too. I could drive to Fred Meyer to do my shopping as an easy drive from the house. The house was on Sehome Hill quite near Western Washington University. Our neighbors on either side were students there, an easy walk away. They never stayed very long. Sometimes they would "borrow" an egg, or get a recipe or something. Our house was built in 1910 or thereabouts, just like the rest of the neighborhood. It was a Greek Revival Prairie style house.

It came time for me to renew my Washington State Driver's License. WOW! It had always been such a simple procedure to renew my driver's license in Longview. Here I was presented with a list of questions to fill out, and required to take a road-test of driving skills. I took the written test, turned it in, then I went on the driving test. I was first required to park on a hill. I thought–I never did have to park on a hill in my life! So I just parked and put on the brake. That was the first mistake. This was the first of FIVE tests–four of which I flunked. I think the last test, they finally let me by simply because they were tired of me and wanted to be rid of me.

My license is still good–despite my problems in obtaining it. I might add that I was ready to give up every time I failed; but Cynthia just said, "No, no! Don't give up!" I had to practice parking and things between tests. We each had a car parked in the back, but we had no garage. There was a carriage house there originally, but we tore it down to give ourselves a place to park. Parking can be a problem in a college neighborhood. I parked in a handicapped parking spot at Fred Meyers, and my "Handicapped-Parking Emblem" had expired. I got a ticket for that. It cost me some money. I needed a doctor's recommendation to get another one, so I used Dr. Kirkpatrick in Longview. I found an osteopathic physician near the house and got an exam there. He was retiring at the time. I had a bad cold one day and was afraid of getting pneumonia again, but he reassured me that it was only a cold. I have not been to a doctor since.

I have a real problem with foot care. I went to a doctor in Longview, when I lived there, to get my toenails trimmed, so I looked for a foot doctor in Bellingham. I made my first (and last) appointment. At the office of Dr.Larrabee, I was given a lengthy questionnaire of my medical history. They even weighed me, took blood type, etc. So finally he got around to trimming my toenails, and then presented me with a bill for $69! From then on I had my beautician, Jan, do my toenails.

We had a lot of visitors in Bellingham, Peg Miller on her way to a Canadian canoe outing, Lee McMurry, the Mullins family, various members of the family, Sue Hinshaw, the opera singer. From London,

Shahram Etemad came with Mansour Jahanmir. Hamid came from Hawaii, also, with his cousin, Mansour. Farshid Jahanmir came to go to the Chinese Medicine clinic which did such a good job with Ted. The Jackson Clinic in Richmond, B.C. did wonders for him. He learned about it from Sam. Sammy and Jessica Chang have the New Peking Restaurant (Chinese) right in our neighborhood. Ted ate there quite a bit when he was working on the house, and remained a loyal customer. He went there, ordered, then went in the restroom and cleaned himself up when there was no kitchen or functional bathroom at the house. They became "family." Sam gave him a map of how to find the clinic and the telephone number. We were there at the Jackson Clinic for an appointment one day when there was an earthquake. Ted and I were on the acupuncture tables when the building began to shake. They must have never been in an earthquake before. They were scared and did not know what to do. We had been in earthquakes before, and this one was not too strong, so we were not scared.

Robin Felper developed physical problems. His kidneys seemed to be shutting down. Ted took him to the Jackson Clinic. It was quite a painful experience for him, as he was very sensitive in the sympathetic acupuncture areas that required needles. He went on dialysis for a while. He came over one Saturday and brought some gingersnaps. He wanted to talk to Ted who was gone. I told him to come back on Monday. When Monday came, he never showed up. He had taken an apartment from Edward on the mainland. When he did not answer the telephone, Edward went over there to see what was up. Robin had been dead since Sunday. Sandra was not worth much for a while. There was no official Memorial Service. Some of his friends got together for closure. Of course I was there, as I was the last one to see him alive. We found out that his ex-wife, who was in California, is Anna Miller, the daughter of Martha Boentgen who was Anne Hillman's teacher and an artist in her own right. It seemed such a small world.

When winter came, Brian Wasson came to see us. We met him at the bus depot, I think. We planned to go to Belize. We drove to SeaTac airport and parked the car, boarded the plane, and stopped in Houston. I had a "wheelchair/disabled" ticket, which made the footwork through airports easier. We arrived in Belize City in the late afternoon. Mario was there at the airport to meet us. He brought his brother, Miguel, and his son, little Jesse, who was a babe in arms the last time we saw him in the U.S.A. Mario brought a car. There was just too much to put in it–people, luggage, and all, so we also hired a taxi and we went to Belmopan.

Miguel did not believe that we existed until he actually saw us with his own eyes. He wanted to be sure that Jesse saw us and stayed fresh in his mind. We went for dinner at the Bullfrog. It is very dark in Belmopan when the sun goes down. As we were leaving the restaurant, we were greeted at the door by his honor, Mayor Anthony Chanona, who gave me a special welcome to the city. Old age has its rewards. We also met his assistant Clifton Hall, who showed up a lot of times in odd places. Apparently the Bullfrog is a meeting place for government people after work. The next morning we took Miguel and Jesse to the border so that they could go home to Guatamala. They went through; we stayed in Belize. This was shortly before Christmas; they probably wanted to be home for the holidays.

We went back to Belmopan and picked up our stuff. It was daylight, so we could see the town. Then we took the Hummingbird Highway to Blue Hole Park, which was closed, so we went on to Dangriga. There was a bakery there that we could smell. We had a bad time trying to find a place to eat. Poor choices, but something had to do. On the way back to the hotel we came across a street full of black people in costume celebrating. These were Garifuna people, an ethnic group in Belize. We went on to bed and during the night a couple next to the hotel bickered and argued all night. She was real mad at him. They both did a lot of yelling, but she punctuated her diatribe by breaking all of their dishes–one at a time. Somewhere around 4 o'clock in the morning, they apparently ran out of china, reached a compromise, or both. All was quiet for the duration.

Next morning we got some bread and vegetables and hit the road again going south. We stopped at the butterfly farm, fed some little fish in the little stream nearby with some of the bread. We passed acres and acres of orange groves. We found a place that we could cross the ditch and pick a few. It was not easy to get at them. There are bananas everywhere. In the commercial orchards, each cluster of bananas is in a blue plastic bag. We came to the end of the asphalt and continued on gravel for a while. Then we came to asphalt again and continued to Punta Gorda, where we found a place to spend the night.

The boys went swimming in the ocean across the street. I decided to take a shower. There was a step up to the shower and a step up to the toilet in that bathroom. I enjoyed the shower–nice warm water on my back. When I stepped out on the first step, it was slick, and I slipped and fell. I did not break any bones, but there I was wet, naked, and down without any way to get up. I managed to get a small towel around me so I could slide myself on that slippery tile floor into the bedroom. I thought I might be able to pry myself up using the foot of the bed and a chair nearby. I had the towel around my shoulders. I tried desperately to get up, but I couldn't. Soon the boys got back and got me back on my feet again. I went to bed and the boys went to see the Garifunas and their show. We checked out and went to another place.

We went in search of an arboretum so that we could see what a mahogany tree looked like, but could not find one that was open. It was closed. We went on, to Columbia, a little village which had been destroyed by a hurricane. Now the entire village was rebuilt. It was square and plumb–unlike the average Belizean village. We explored it. There was a concrete building. It had withstood the hurricane. Everyone came into it during the storm. Ted was impressed with the acoustics, so Mario got his guitar and did an impromptu recital there. The acoustics were indeed good. Soon people began to appear at the windows just to listen. I noticed how simple the people live. You see chickens in nearly every yard, sometimes a pig, and wonder how they make a living. We were looking for a Mennonite farm, and stopped at a place and asked about it. He told us a lot about them. They raise rice there.

We went on to the Blue River, a lovely park along beside the river. Women and children selling stuff were everywhere. Then we went back to our new hotel. It was the best place yet for me. I had a water bed and plenty of covers to keep warm. The Caribbean Sea was just across the road. We had dinner and breakfast there and a very pleasant visit with the proprietor, a local history teacher. He told us a great deal about the Garifuna people and their pageants.

On the way out of town, we stopped at the gas station where we bought gas before. Again we bought gas, went on for a way, and decided that we would do well to check the tires, so we turned around and went back. We bought a couple of tires. A person there knew about Mario's school, Galileo University. His brother went there. Mario's student card has opened doors for him on several occasions. With two new tires we went on to the Blue Hole Park on the road we traversed before. The boys went in. Mario and Brian swam there. There was a cave there. Mario and Ted went into it, but Brian would not enter. As I was waiting for the cavers in the parking lot, I used a very unusual rest room. The entry was up stairs.

We went back to Belmopan. Our next trip was back on the Western Highway again. We went to Benque Viejo. We had lunch at a place there on the road and were almost harassed by a local sculptor who was rather offensive. Brian bought something. There was a pretty river right there across the road. We went through the Guatemala border and got on one of the worst roads of the region. We went to Florez, Guatemala. It was Christmas Eve. We found a hotel on an island of a lake. Ted bought blankets so that we would have something to keep us warm at night. Intermittent fire works were going on like the 4th of July–extremely loud. We had dinner at the Mayan Restaurant: First, soup, then, venison, beef, and took leftovers with us. We called Marina. She would be gone to the beach on Christmas Day. We went on to bed. The fireworks got louder and faster. Finally about 2 in the morning things started to simmer down so we could get some sleep. Christmas Day the streets were just covered with spent firecrackers which blew around in every little breeze. What a mess!

We went on to Rio Dulce and saw a serious accident on the way. Christmas morning we saw a red car on its side. We must have been the first car that passed since it landed. One man lay on the ground as if dead. Another walked around bleeding profusely with severe head wounds, dazed. Horsemen approached driving cows toward the gate on the road. They held back the cows and came over. A car or two stopped by this time. Ted got the bleeding man with a shirt on his head to slow the blood flow. Somebody must have had a cell phone, so we left. We went on our way, and stopped for breakfast. It was a very pleasant place across the road from the Seventh Day Adventist Church. The people had already heard about the accident and knew the men involved. They were locals. The lady reminded us of Peg Miller, so we called it Peg Miller's restaurant. No English was spoken, but the food was extra good.

On to Guatemala City--the air pollution is extreme. We saw the conservatory, parks, palace, beautiful buildings and Mario's school, Galileo University. It was a big, busy, crowded city, and we moved right along to Antigua, a former capital. We went on to Chemultengo, where we met the couple who took care of Mario when he was in recovery from getting hit by the car and having a pin installed in his hip. We spent the night in a hotel there. There was a grassy yard there where we saw a very exotic bird–a scarlet macaw–just wild there in a tree the next morning. Then we saw Mario's high school and walked around there. We went on to Huehuetenengo. We stopped to exchange some money there, and started up the hills.

It started to get cooler as we gained altitude in the mountains. We were on our way to San Juan Ixcoy where Mario had family. It was a frightening ascent–such crooked, torturous, roads. When we were on a plateau we saw farms, a little boy tending a flock of sheep, and other places with more sheep, stone fences. This area was sparsely populated and lots of rocks. From the top of the hill we could see where we would be going. It was an incredibly deep valley with huge mountains on every side. A marker nearby was a place where a family coming home in the dark went over the edge and down the precipice. They were all killed. We could see a waterfall far below and on the other side. This was a place where locals stop and pass water on a standing rock. We met the mayor of San Juan Ixcoy doing exactly that while we were there. Going down the hill, toward the river the road was extremely rough, narrow, and tortuous, with hairpin turns. I don't know what people did who met a car going the opposite direction.

We passed through San Juan Ixcoy on our way to Quesil, the little village where Mario's parents lived. We got to the bottom of the valley, crossed the river, and followed the road to the end and parked the car. The stream was clear and nice. It was late in the afternoon. The men walked with Mario to visit his mother. It was too far for me to walk. I waited in the car. I watched some little boys playing around. It got darker, and they went into their houses. Finally they came back with Mario's mother, Isobel, and his little brothers and sisters. Neither of us knew a word of the others language, so we just threw our arms around each other and hugged. We said good-bye and went on down the road again.

We stopped to see a grandparent at a house. On the outside, the house looked pretty good. When we went in, it was different. There was a stove unlike any stove that I ever saw. It was made out of concrete blocks with a metal lid over the top of the firebox, so you could cook on it. It was also used for heat. The grandmother was sitting beside the stove. The floor was unbelievably dirty. She would spit on the floor kind of over to the side. There was not really a place to sit down. Everyone else stayed afoot. I was in desperation. I asked to use the bathroom, because it had been quite a while. I'll never forget how primitive that place was. They took me out in back of the house where there was a back porch built over the river. There was a kind of a cement 'stool' with a hole in the top so that was where you sat to pee in the river. There was no "toilet" at all. There was no door to go through. It was like outside. I was escorted by a girl or two or I would have never made it. They brought me a roll of toilet paper. Just to think of it makes me laugh. That was the oddest thing.

We left and went back to spend the night in San Juan Ixcoy in a hotel. We were now on our way to visit Marina in El Salvador. We re-negotiated the mountains up and down, Huehuetenengo, and all to head south from Chemultenengo. We went to Lago Isabel. The sun was going down over across the lake, the sky and water were dramatic yellow which faded into orange; it was very pretty. There was a big volcano very prominent in the landscape. We saw it from many sides. Unfortunately we did not stay there in that lovely place. We looked around and went on to Escuinta, which seemed a likely place at the time. We found a hotel and went in to see the rooms. The plumbing was painted a dark magenta and there was the biggest cockroach that we encountered. Rather than staying there, we went back to a motel on the outskirts of town.

Next day we went over the El Salvador border and drove into San Salvador and called Marina. We told her where we were, and Marina and company came to escort us to their palatial home. It really was a palace. It looked like something from the early Hollywood type architecture that you might expect to see in Sunset Boulevard. There were gardens and pools, totally neglected because there was no gardener any more. She had a large lovely poinsettia on one side of the house, many exotic trees with fruit, banana grove and everything. The ceilings were very high so that the house was cool. They still had servants to do the cooking and cleaning. They were going to make it into a hotel, but there was some sort of problem with it. This place was where Marina grew up. It was passed on to her sister who was many years older and had predeceased everyone else. Now the house belonged to the son of her sister, a graduate of Harvard or Stanford. His English was as good as mine. He lived there with his wife and two daughters. We spent the afternoon. Mario played the guitar in the big room with the high ceiling, and sounded really good. It was nice to use a toilet and not worry.

We continued on through the border into Honduras where we spent the night–Acaltepeque. We got a free breakfast. It was a nice place. From Honduras we crossed into Guatemala. We stopped to buy stamps at Esquipulas, Guatemala. We saw the Cathedral of the Black Jesus. Then we went on to Zacapa where we bought a watermelon. Then we went on to Rio Dulce where we spent the rest of the afternoon and night. Bowels moved here. I had a problem with constipation. Sitting all the time is not good. It was like a youth camp beside the river. It was rustic, but comfortable. We all slept in one room with lots of beds. There is a lake there with a lot of boats on it. There is a big bridge over it. We met an old man, Bob, from Las Vegas who spent every winter there. There was also a cultural snob here from Spain who couldn't stand local Spanish. Purists come in all flavors.

The next morning we got back on the road to Belize and stopped for breakfast at Peg Miller's little restaurant again. We found out that the guys who were in the wreck on Christmas Day, were all still alive.

They did not want the authorities to know about this accident. From the number of armed servicemen who stood around carrying AK-47's, we could understand why the locals would not want the authorities involved with anything.

We went on to Belmopan for the night, and the next day we started off for the Zoo. We drove for a while until we knew we had passed it without knowing it. We stopped about 11:00 A.M. at a restaurant run by Marva Gillette. There was no crowd yet, so we visited with her. She and her sister had cottages to rent that were completely furnished. She took us to one that was not occupied. This was around Hattieville. It was lovely, except that it was a LONG way to a grocery store, and we would not have a car without Mario. As long as we were this close to Belize City, Mario drove in and bought a towel for Jesse and we looked around a little. We continued back toward Belmopan and watched for the Zoo. It was late afternoon when we got into it. They were getting close to closing it. It was a remarkable place. They had the native birds and animals where we could see them–in VERY LARGE cages. They had a raised platform to view the tapirs because they would use their urine as a weapon and let you have it if they could. They also had elevated platforms for birds. Then we went back to Belmopan.

The next day we checked out of Belmopan and went on our way to Belize City. We were trying to get to San Pedro, but the last vessel had gone. We parked our car and entrusted it to a local man who said that he would watch it. He assured us that we could find a place to stay on Caye Caulker, so we took luggage and boarded a motorboat with a bunch of other people. It was rather crowded. We went out into the Caribbean for a distance and after while we arrived at the dock. We were there for a couple days. Our landlady came with a golf cart and picked us up with luggage. It was very near the dock and overlooked the Sea. Brian camped in the yard, and it rained in the middle of the night. It was more than a little rain; it poured. It blew up into the porch furniture and filled the seats. Brian decided to spend the rest of the night inside after all.

It was the day of New Year's Eve. We got a golf cart and buzzed around exploring. We saw the generator that provided electricity for the island. We saw the graveyard, and the residential district where people who worked there lived. There were a lot more hotels in proportion to residences. Festivities were in preparation for New Year's Eve. Lots of people milling around—there was a big restaurant that had sand on the floor. It was part walled, and part open, and another place where they played Vivaldi. We went back to Vega and went to bed. Another night of fireworks and frivolity met our ears. It was not much in the way of noise compared to Christmas in Florez.

Patricia came in to clean the room the next morning. We had a hard time finding a place to eat breakfast because it was a holiday and everyone was pretty well partied out. We did find a place that was on stilts like traditional Belizean architecture. Then we went to the dock with our luggage to await the ferry (motorboat); a gusty wind blew my high-rise toilet seat right off of the dock and into the bay. The wind kept blowing and—the toilet seat got blown toward the shore. Mario ran around there and retrieved it. The box was a little soggy, but it was okay. Getting in and out of the boat was really difficult for me. Brian pretty well picked me up and hauled me in and out of it. We got dropped at the dock and got in the car. Mario took us to the airport, and left us there. We waited for the plane and he went on back to Guatemala.

We arrived in Seattle and it was snowing. It had been snowing for some time. The be-turbaned taxi-driver did not know how to drive in snow and was frightened by it, but did take us to our car. We went back home to Bellingham all the way in the snow. Later, I got a call from the Bellingham airport saying that we had a package there waiting for us. We did not want to go anywhere in the snow, so we waited to get it for some time. Brian left for Lewis County on the bus. When the snow melted, we went out to the airport and picked up the well-traveled toilet seat.

Ted went back to school at Bellingham Technical College. It was the same place where we went to get our teeth cleaned, in the dental department. Ted was taking cooking. I could get transportation from the City of Bellingham if I requested it the day before. This day I went to the dental department at the school. When I was through there one of the girls took me over to the cooking department and cafeteria where Ted was. And I had lunch there before going home. I forgot what I had, but it was good.

There was a Presbyterian Church just down the hill a few blocks from the house–on Garden Street. I decided to go there and see what it was like. I was disappointed, the people were unfriendly, and I did not care for the Pastor, a woman. The Baptist church was closer, but had become a gymnasium for martial arts. It was Bernadine Hershell in Latah who advised me where to go to church. She once lived in Ferndale. The people in this church I think supported her through a painful divorce. She gave me the name of a person to ask for there, and I did. It was Emmanuel Bible Church, and it became my church home. The people were friendly, the music was excellent, and they had busses to pick up riders for their services. The bus came to my house to the back door every Sunday morning, so I had many friends in the church.

The last summer that we were in Bellingham, Ted fell down over at Lake Padden while running around it, and went to the hospital. Edward went to the hospital and brought him home. At the time he was telling me about his driving. He said that he quit driving, and he forgot how. Even though his eyesight was not very good, as he was blind in one eye due to a stroke, he was just going to keep right on driving so that he would never have to learn how again. Ted wore a bandage for a long time, but the bone that the hospital thought was broken was NOT broken. Since he had horse manure in the wound, however, it was serious. He had actually broken it a few years ago and the Xray could not tell if it was a fresh break or an old one. We just waited it out. It was a deep cut that required cleaning and stitches.

Ted was interested in baking school, and there was no piano work for him thanks to September 11th, but Bellingham Tech quit offering baking. So he looked at Olympia, Tacoma, and Vancouver. The best choice was in Vancouver. We planned to move to Randle where we had a remodel in progress. It just never seemed to get ready. It was supposed to be done in May or June. Here it was summertime. We moved plants down there, put in an orchard and garden, so the dahlias were installed there. Still, the house was not ready, and they quit working on it. I was supposed to live there in the house, and Ted would be in school 4 days a week and come back home during days off until he got out of school. That way on completion he could start a bakery there. The time came to move, the house was for sale, so we were obliged to find other living quarters.

Ted went to Vancouver to look for a little rat-hole where he could sleep three nights a week. In the process he found a house near the campus and figured that he could re-sell it after school. In a pinch, I could live there too until the house at Randle was done. Mike invited me to spend some time with him and took the train. He took the afternoons off from his job at the office and we went to gardens where they showed all the many different kinds of plants that grew in Oregon. We went to see his horses at the horse barn. Another afternoon we went to the Vista House on Columbia Gorge. That was the original highway through the Oregon side of the

Columbia Gorge. This old road was the way that I had come to Portland with Bob and Ruth to the "Camp Meeting" when I was a high-school girl.

Another afternoon we came to Vancouver to see the house that Ted bought. We went on north for a long way, and realized that we had overshot the destination. Then we came back around and found it. When I got back to Bellingham, Sandra had sold the house, and we had to move out of Bellingham. The house in Randle was still not ready, so both of us had to move into the Vancouver house. We took possession on October 1, 2004. The house was not much, so we decided to winter in Belize again because there was no central heat–among other things. Cynthia was here at the time of our moving in and she stayed in the basement and used the bathroom there beside her room. All was well at the time. About the next week we had a major sewage back-up down there. Mike came over and put some stuff on it and tried to make it go away. It persisted, and seeped into all the basement rooms. That was just the beginning of our house problems in Vancouver. We had not yet unpacked; and now, this. Plumbers got involved and ran a camera down the line. The whole basement floor had to be taken out and new drains put in. I spent a lot of time over at Mike's.

We went to Belize and left Dorothy Hopkins in charge of the house. It was good to stop huddling around the little electric wall heater in the dining room every night. Mario met us at the Belize airport again this trip. We went back to the El Rey Inn, and found a house to rent for several months–# 19 Swasey Street. It became our home for this time. It was rather unusually arranged because between the kitchen and dining room, was the washer and dryer, and also a liquor bar and bar stools. From the dining room was a living room, part of which was down a few steps which must have been a converted garage. The television set and the telephone were in that room. From the dining room were the three south bedrooms and bath. My bedroom and bath were on the north side. There was an odd storage room that looked like it should have been the laundry or dining nook or part of the kitchen. The backyard had a grapefruit tree with fruit on it, banana, and tangerine without fruit.

A watchdog in the front yard, named Dreen, came with the house. She was a large, black, smooth-haired Belizean dog. First she had to learn not to keep us out of the house. By the time we left, Ted had her pretty well trained so that she would take commands, sit, stay, heel, etc. The neighborhood children were impressed. Apparently nobody there trains their dog to do anything except yowl with all the other dogs every night. She also passed a period of estrus which had a lot of male dogs interested. Ticks were a problem there and she attracted them. Sometimes you would see ticks just walking around on the patio taking a stroll. Ants there are small but aggressive. In the road was what was left of a tarantula that was being eaten by them. It is warm there, so they move faster than they do in the north where they are cool and slow.

One day at the market in Belmopan a vehicle came by manned by Chinese-Belizeans who were inviting people apparently at random to their Christmas party. This was a Chinese Christian Church. It was Christmas; we had no other offers, so we went. It was a dinner program. First was dinner. You went around there and got as much or as little as you wanted as many times as you wanted to. We met a medical person from out of town who advised us on how to eat. He said to start with fruit, then move to vegetables, then move to starch and meat. This was all Chinese food excellently prepared in massive quantities with a lot of different choices. After dinner they moved all the dinner, leftovers, and traces of dinner out of the area. Then the program started with a little stage with a curtain on it at the back of the place. The curtain was not very secure. They would open and close it very tentatively. They sang, they spoke etc. all in Chinese. They nursed the curtain through the evening. There was a little boy who played the violin who was from Taiwan living there with his aunt to learn English. Most everyone else spoke Chinese, so we were alone in the crowd. It was a very interesting Christmas–very nice people.

After we settled in there we went to Tikal (Guatemala) with Mario driving his little pick-up. We took the same horrible gravel road into Guatemala that we traversed before. We explored Tzikintzakan, a little known archeological site along this road. Mario said that tzakan means "bird" in Mayan. We have no clue as to what kind of bird or what the rest of the word means. The boys went up the hill, I sat in the car. Nobody was there. I was alone in the parking lot.

The boys came back and we pressed on to Tikal. Tikal has a paved road to it. The road signs said that the animals had the right of way, so we were to watch out for them on the highway. We found a parking lot full of cars and people. They had all sorts of vehicles there and even a little airport. It was truly a big deal. We had to get up the hill. A taxi came and ferried me up the hill. The boys walked. There was a big open space with all those pyramids around. They made human sacrifices there at specific places that were designed to hold the blood of the victims. There were many people who met their end right in this place. The boys climbed around a lot, but I sat there and looked. Hundreds of people were around there. Many different languages were spoken by guides to groups of visitors.

I also was ferried out of there and sat and waited at the entrance under a tree. There was a place to sit. I counted the people as they streamed by in and out of there. In the hour that I sat there, there must have been two or three hundred people until I got tired counting and listened to birds. Restrooms there are interesting. I needed to find one before we went on. We did go on, not back. Mario saw a little road while they were walking down the hill, and he drove over and took it. He got permission to go on it–Uaxatun, which was even more remote than Tikal, a dead-end road going north from Tikal into the jungle. This was the most undeveloped area that we encountered. It was a little gravel one-lane road with occasional turn-outs. We picked up a guy who was walking. He was picking medicinal herbs out in the jungle, and going home for dinner. He had us stop and listen to the monkeys, and they all climbed a forest look-out tower just off the road a way. The car was just parked in the middle of the road for a while as there was absolutely no traffic. We got to Uaxatun, and he got out and went to a house. He told us where the ruins were and we went there. It was not developed either.

It was late in the day and we were on our way back out again through the village and we saw a tree full of oranges with fruit on the ground and everything. When we stopped to pick some, the people who lived there told us that they were not edible. We do not know why, but that is how it was. They were ornamental. We met a jeep with Dutch people in it when we were on the way out. We went back to the motel and were hungry for dinner and went downtown in Santa Elena. It was an outdoor cafe. The man was on the sidewalk in front with halved chickens that he was barbequing. He did the main courses. The woman was the vegetables. The son was beverages. He had a bucket full of oranges and a hand juicer. Mario ordered the chicken, rice, beans, etc. The most unusual part of the scene was that they were quarreling and angry with each other. They were very pleasant to us, but not to each other. The food was wonderful and there was a lot of it. When we were low, they just brought more so it was all we could eat. We gave a nice tip, hugged and thanked them, and asked them to please be happy, and they reconciled. We went back for breakfast, but they were closed.

We went back on the same tortuous road to Belize again. Mario's insurance would expire the next day and he would have to go back to Guatemala, so he did. Without Mario we had no transportation, so we bought a bicycle at Oscar Chu's Bicycle shop and had it outfitted with baskets for carrying groceries, etc. Oscar, his real name is He, became quite a good friend. He was trained as a Chinese doctor in Taiwan and had been around. He explained the difference between mainland Chinese and Taiwanese Chinese. His wife, Ai-ling, was the trained bicycle business, and she pitched right in. They have two children, a girl, Kaolee Yagami, who is in high school, and a boy younger. She played some kind of Chinese stringed instrument–zither?–for us with traditional Chinese Classical music. They want to hear Ted play piano, and have him lined up as soon as they open their medical tourism resort.

Lorna and her daughter, Alex, came after New Year's. She had a Sabbatical leave from Hillsdale College. I had gone to visit them in Hillsdale, Michigan, on two different occasions. Once on a Thanksgiving weekend in the 1990's; then when Alex graduated from high school, I went there for her graduation party. She graduated at a younger age than the average student. I met her grandparents there. They planned to take her to Italy to see her father, and also to Ireland where they must have had ancestors. I always wondered why Sylvia never would go and visit them. Alex was supposed to go to England to go to school. She visited Oxford, but she was quite unhappy there and wanted to come home, so she was with Lorna at this time–and with us in Belmopan.

Then Cynthia also came in January. Ted went on the bus to meet her at the airport. The bus, however, did not go to the airport. He ended up in Orange Walk in north Belize while she waited for him. She called up and I told her I did not know where he actually was, but he was trying to get there. She rented a car and waited around and they both got together and came home. She was there for about 10 days. With a car, the girls could go places and went to the beach at Placencia for a few days, saw Xunantunich, the zoo and things. We looked at pictures of our time at the zoo. I sat on a bench and looked down a road into the zoo. I talked to the taxi-driver parked next to us. He asked if I spoke English. He was taking a group back to the Belize airport and they stopped there on the way. He wanted us to know that if we needed transportation, he would be available back in Belmopan. Cynthia took pictures of the zoo and all, and showed them to us. There was a picture of an old lady walking up the path–couldn't see her face. I said. "She's got my hat on! Oh! It's me!"

When it was time for us to come back to USA, we packed up all our stuff at #19 Swasey Street–dishes, sheets, bedding, cooking utensils, and cleaned the house. Oscar took a break from selling his home-grown orchids and fixing bikes, and found another place for us to rent at half the price on Garbutt Creek Street, a Chinese community. He took us over to see it. It was nice, with high ceilings, quiet street, nice amenities.

It was underneath another residence. We had the main floor. We liked it and took it. We left our stuff right there–including the elevated toilet seat in a wooden traveling box. We paid a few months' rent. Then, when it was time, he took us to the airport and we came back to the United States to Portland.

Mike met us in the middle of the night and took us to his place to stay. When we went over to see the house again, it was just a total mess! We spent some time with Mike. Then I took off to stay with Cynthia for a while. The mess seemed to go on forever. We expected the house to be in a LOT better shape than it was. We had to get a different contractor to finish the house because the one we had was such a drone. That was how we met John Younkin. He worked for the other guy, so we hired him directly and he got a license to be a contractor himself and do it all. It was a beginning for him. He had done it all, and knew it all. Now he did it his way, and enjoyed it.

At last the car is parked in the garage. The house is finished, insulated inside and out, and very comfortable. We are close to the grocery store–across the street–close to the library, Post Office, downtown, and the airport is a quick easy taxi ride away. We are close to everything. The lawn and gardens are lovely.

Mike had a big birthday party for his father in Madras, Oregon, when he turned 90. It was a beautiful trip over there; the weather was warm and nice. We drove there and were the first ones there so that the piano could get tuned a little if needed. We saw all of Mike's family together for the event. Since the house was not done, we did not return to Belize the next winter. Instead, Mike married Joanie on December 8th of 2005. This time we journeyed to Mount Hood to a resort where they said their vows. Again the family was assembled for dinner and dancing. We came home rather than staying overnight. It started snowing before we left and we got lost getting out of there. Home looked pretty good that night even though it was not finished yet. Summer of 2006 Mike's father, who is a diabetic, had a serious medical problem. He must have had a mild stroke; the result was a blood clot in his foot. They wanted to amputate. He declined and was transferred to the Veterans Hospital down the street a few blocks. He was close to us, so we visited him frequently. I could go there pushed in a wheelchair. He returned home with his foot attached to his body. Now, unfortunately, Mike has a serious medical problem–prostate cancer.

Our landlord in Belmopan got a divorce and had to move into our house on Garbutt Creek Street himself. Oscar He took our stuff over to the bicycle shop and stored it overhead. They have been building a house in a new part of town and were going to change the location of themselves, the shop, and all. He had acreage to build a medical vacation spot. Meanwhile, we do not have a place to stay when we get there, but Keith might find us a place in Ontario Village, or Esther (Meili Lu) asked if she should help us find a place, too.

On our last trip to Longview to take care of my income tax, we had time to explore Coal Creek. So we went to see Larry Wilson. My! How the area has grown since we lived there. The fields are full of homes. But Larry is at the very end of the road and owns considerable land there. He inherited Celia Bean's house, cleaned it up, and with considerable expense made it beautiful. He is afraid to rent it out, it might get spoiled. So he goes there to read the newspaper. He was doing canning in his mother's home and extracting honey over at his house. His mother was such a good friend to me. I took her to town for dinner once and I went up there to visit often. She told me about her life when she first came to Longview and worked for the rich Vandercooks, and how she persuaded her husband to buy the land up there—it was cheap. If our farm had stayed the end of the road like Larry's—how different life would have been.

Epilogue

The Moving Finger writes; and, having writ,
Moves on: nor all thy Piety nor Wit
Shall lure it back to cancel half a Line,
Nor all thy Tears wash out a Word of it.

Omar Khayyam
(E. Fitzgerald, translator)

www.ingramcontent.com/pod-product-compliance
Lightning Source LLC
Chambersburg PA
CBHW061956090426

42811CB00006B/959